CONNECTING

G◯D
A
N
D
Y◯U

CONNECTING

GOD AND YOU

Laurence Lilley

Connecting God And You

Copyright © 2013 Laurence Lilley

Published by: Wynthru Publishing, Australia

ABN: 22 057 003 198
ISBN: 978-0-9873850-1-7

Printed in Australia
www.laurencelilleysbooks.com

Scripture quotations are taken from the Amplified' Bible, Copyright ©
1954, 1958, 1962, 1964, 1965, 1987 by The Lockman Foundation.
Used by permission. *www.Lockman.org*

Cover base photo, NASA, ESA, and S.Beckwith (STSc)
and the HUDF Team. Used with permission.

CONTENTS

WHAT I'M ON ABOUT

I have written and re-written this book so many times there is not much left of the original. The original has actually been published twice with different titles, but was never distributed.

I am glad those versions that went through the publishing process were never distributed. They were written for church people which had me talking about things that would not make a lot of sense to most of us.

This time I am encouraging people who have not been involved with church – or things considered to be religious – to have another look at life. So, we are concentrating on your personal involvement with God – and why that look is highly recommended.

Your connection with God completes you. It's why you were born. You discover the wonder of what God has intended for you while you are here in this life and what he has prepared for what follows.

I know the magnitude of what is really going on is beyond anyone's ability to know – or to be able to tell you – but what I have here is enough to get you thinking and get you involved in the most fantastic life you could ever know.

Anyhow, do read it all. You will find purpose you didn't realise existed.

Laurence

CHAPTER ONE

THE NITTY GRITTY

Let's get right into it and tell you that God and You connecting with each other is the most truly important, consequential, life-purpose-fulfilling event that can ever happen to you.

When I say "God" you know who I am talking about. I am talking about God the Bible talks about. Eternal Creator. God Almighty. Lord God Most High. Our Heavenly Father. Our Dad. Our Big Brother Jesus. Our Friend and Companion Holy Spirit That God. But you know that. The knowing is built into us.

The only authentic factual and indisputable history of the beginning of things is in the Bible. By that I mean, there is no other data to check against. What I'm saying here and occasionally throughout this book is not a sales pitch for the Bible, but what is written there has stood the test of time, and will still stand up to anything anyone likes to throw at it. During the past several hundred years there have been many serious attempts to discredit it by the-very-clever-people.

Most of these are dead, and the Bible is still being sold at the rate of 100 million every year.

So – because this is the only existing history of the way things began, we are going to say that in the very first chapter of the Bible, the indisputable information is that God said. "Let us make a man in our image and after our likeness," – or in plain language – "Let's duplicate ourselves."

God built that man in some location in Iraq. The rivers Euphrates and Tigris (Hidekkel) named in that first chapter giving the location of Eden are a positive identifier and those rivers are still there where they have always been.

Eden was a real place and Adam and Eve were real people. Your very existence backs up what is recorded in those first chapters in the Bible. And – there is no history or solid factual evidence anywhere on Earth able to refute what is recorded there. Whole hurricanes of hot air, but no substance. If you are going to believe something, it is a good idea to base your believing on fact and evidence, not wild guesses. This time – stand in front of a mirror. Your evidence is right there looking at you.

The point is that wherever it occurred, God made a man who was a copy of himself. That man is your very own original grandfather. Adam was a real person – and so was Eve. You are irrefutable evidence that these were both real people.

I am going to say that God built men and women – that God built you – the same species of being he is. God's intention is to have a family of people who are the same species as himself – and he has given us what is needed so that can happen.

It is God's fixed intention that people be the same as he is and we are not much use to him until we are.

There are people squatting in our education establishments and government funded science labs around the world, who, for reasons even they could not explain, go to a great deal of trouble to try to convince you – or even themselves – that you are of not much consequence. Again – let these idiots speak for themselves, but every time you look in the mirror, you know. Every time you see one of the children you have brought into the world – you know. You watch them grow. You watch them become a real person with character and personality and intelligence – that's the product of random development from a dollop of swap goop???? Like – where did the character and personality and intelligence come from???? Let's stop trying to kid ourselves. Let's stop the crap. It's insanity gone mad.

When God Almighty created your original grandparents he made them in "the image and likeness" of himself He made them, and ultimately you – the same species of being he is. No accidents. No swamp goop.

The opening line in the Bible says, "In the beginning God created...." If you don't mind me pointing it out – that is the only irrefutable history in existence that tells us how things that are, came to be.

That first line in the Bible goes on to say, "In the beginning God created the heavens and the earth. And the earth became shapeless and empty and darkness was upon the face of the deep and the Spirit of God was moving over the face of the waters."

That was the conditions on Planet Earth before any restoration had begun. The first chapter of Geneses is not about The Creation-Of-The- World. It is about the restoration of the already existing Planet Earth. That opening line says – Earth was created "in the beginning" – the same time as other major creation projects had been built. We will discover that some of that "beginning" creation was a very, very, very, very long time ago. Like multi billion years ago. God has been at this a very, very, very, very long time.

Most of the first chapter of Genesis is talking about the restoration that week of a badly damaged planet.

The reason that reconstruction had become necessary was that quite a long time ago a problem had erupted at Headquarters. God had been building up his development team for eons; angels and mighty supernatural beings of all classes and specialist abilities.

Archangel Lucifer, the senior member of the Administration Team, decided he wanted to be General Manager and attempted a coup on the incumbent CEO. A hostile take-over. Really hostile. This angel attempted to throw Eternal Creator God Almighty out of Heaven.

One-third of the staff at Headquarters who had been trained and equipped as Executive Management joined in the coup, hoping to secure promotion for themselves in The New Heaven Order.

God Almighty – being that he *IS* God Almighty – it didn't work.

I have never been able to understand how Lucifer imagined he was going to pull it off. That creature must be a truly awesome and powerful being to even *think* he could overthrow his Creator. Something had obviously happened to his ability to think straight. The Bible says that pride was found in him.

Lucifer – also known as "satan" and as "the devil" – and his gang were expelled from Heaven and dumped on little Planet Earth. That was a very long time ago. It could have been millions of years ago. As planets go, Earth is tiny, but the extent of the damage done would have taken a very long time to accomplish.

For billions of eons God Almighty has been working on a program and what he starts, he finishes. Planet Earth is involved. A little thing like a rebellion in Heaven was not going to change anything.

It is time to begin the next stage which is where you show up.

In a few minutes we are going to meet your very great-grand parents.

CHAPTER TWO

YOU SHOW UP

Before we go off to meet your grampa and granma, let's stop for a while and have a big long think. Our Father God had you in mind and loved you and has kept loving you since before time was – before anything was – before he dreamed up what eventually developed into being the massive Creation Project of which we can see a tiny particle in the night sky – before there was Heaven or the Throne Room – before there were angels – before there was a Planet Earth – further back than it is possible for humans to imagine – our Dad had conceived you and had locked you in his heart and he has loved you ever since way back then. Before anything was, Our Family –- Our Dad – Our Big Brother – Our Friend and Companion Holy Spirit – were out there setting things up and getting things ready for you. You are not an idea tacked on to the end of The Creation Project – The Project is tacked on to the end of your Father's heart-yearning intentions for you. Our Family thinks big – and they are thinking of you as that project is coming together.

In the next chapter I am going to start telling you that God made you like he is so you can be as he is and do as he does. You are the most significant creature our Father Creator God ever made, Everything that exists is put together with you in mind.

OK – at this time in HisStory – Stage One of The Project is complete.

Human people are made to be the Executive Principals of Creation Stage Two. Father God made us so Creation can be brought to life – to spread his glory throughout the Universe – to give point and purpose to the existence of the limitless enormousness of what he has made.

Galaxies – massive stars – atoms – it's all there just to let you catch a glimpse of the magnitude and mind-frying complexity of this Family of ours and what has been prepared for you. With his Love and Power and Glory flooding out from within us and filling Creation with Life and Purpose – this is going to be a long term – a very long term – very exciting adventure and a lot of fun.

Everything we are involved with at this time in history is sitting in the middle of Eternity. Eternity behind us has produced all the stuff – and us – and our Creator Dad has made us – you – ready for what he has planned. Eternity ahead is for us – for you – to be bringing the stuff to life. The whole point of Creation is so we can spread Father's love and his glory throughout all that exists. We are the containers – we are the carriers and spreaders of that glory. It flows out from us through all creation. We are not made for just messing around on this planet as we are messing around on this planet – we are Father's dream. We are his kids – his boys and girls – and yea verily – his administrators and developers – and he is watching us enjoy what he has been building for us since before time ever was. Our Family takes us very seriously.

It's time to meet Grandpa and Grandma.

Our physical involvement began when the Creation Team arrived here several thousand years ago. Planet Earth had already been here for a very long time – soil was here – atmosphere was here – water was here. It was all messed up, but it was already in existence. Earth was NOT created as part of that five day restoration. The Bible history is that Earth was created "in the beginning" – which was a very long time ago. Any of you CS folk reading this – get your facts right. Your stuff is even more absurd than that other lot.

Archangel Cherub Lucifer and his gang had been dumped out here when expelled from Headquarters as the consequence of attempting that coup on God Almighty. In a mindless, furious, destructive rampage they had trashed the planet, reducing it to a shapeless, flooded, empty mess. We can understand a bit of their frustrated rage. These creatures were top brass in Heaven. Lucifer, a created being, held a position of such power and authority he even imagined he could overthrow Eternal Creator God Almighty who had made him. From many ages of enjoying an environment we can't even relate to – here they are stuck in the mud and muck of the pigsty they had created. Instead of basking in the radiant glory suffusing Heaven – it's pitch dark. They have blown it, and it's for keeps. Which wasn't a very smart thing to do. They are very unhappy campers.

Holy Spirit spent considerable time inspecting the damage and mess Lucifer and his cohorts had created and for several weeks brooded – "incubated", which takes time – over the entire planet setting it up for reconstruction.

It's Sunday morning, the first day. The thick heavy cloud cover is dispersed. Darkness was on "*the face of the deep*" – not universal – and on water on Earth, not somewhere in deep space. The light which had been streaming from our Sun since the beginning broke through and Planet Earth is all lit up once more and the working week is under way. Light was not invented that Sunday morning. Light has been streaming from our sun in this "solar system" constellation of our Milky Way galaxy for a very long time. Light that is visible from Planet Earth has been streaming from distant galaxies for thousands and millions and billions of years.

By near end of that week the planet has been refurbished and re-regulated ready for the new creature to move in and take possession.

Genesis 1 is largely the account of repairing the damage these galoots had produced on Planet Earth. After having spent billions of eons building billions of galaxies, including our Milky Way – simply getting the lights working again, cleaning up the atmosphere, re-shaping the surface topography and returning the water to its seabeds, re-vegetating, re-stocking, resetting the timing sequences on this tiny planet was not a very big deal.

Now for the exciting part. The point of the whole exercise.

It is Friday morning in the year – which according to the Jewish calendar – the Jewish people are very good at this kind of thing – was Jewish Year 1 or BCY "Before Civil Year" 3760 – or our Western calendar reckoning 3760 BC – "Before Christ" – or 5773 years ago as this is being written in 2013 AD – standing together wherever Eden was in Iraq – Eternal Creator God Almighty spoke –

"Let us duplicate ourselves." If you can make "in our image and after our likeness" to mean anything else – please tell me about it.

They are excited. This is a huge adventure. The point and purpose of all this creative construction project they have been working on for the past several billion eons is about to happen and to be this close to the culmination of all that hard work would make anyone excited.

Making Adam was not a "let there be man *POOF* and Adam was" job. It seems they spent the whole day on this one.

Creator God gathers a few buckets of clay and with their own bare hands pat the mud ball into the shape of their own being. This is Eternal Creator God Almighty doing that patting.

With the force that brought all Creation into existence being infused into that mud shape with every pat, the atomic structure that had formed the clay is being altered and realigned and redeployed and recombined. Every atom and molecule begins to oscillate and vibrate as the life energy flowing from the hand of Creator God hits it. It is changing. It is no longer clay. Its elemental molecular structure is being diverted and recombining and rearranging into forming human body cell building components, multiple trillions of them.

The living blueprint of the life of God himself – all God Almighty is – Eternal Creator's DNA – is being imparted into each component of those new cells as that Life Force surges through that clay man.

The organs and plumbing begin to form and take shape. Arteries and veins have formed. Bone cells make bones and kidney cells make kidneys. Brain cells form brain. Nerve cells build electrical circuitry cabling. Eye cells form the incredible video cameras that are our eyes. Flesh and muscle cells build flesh and muscle. Skin cells make skin. Hair cells make hair. Holy Spirit is having the time of his life like a boy with a new train set, switching and shunting and crossing over and setting signals and coordinating all the bits and pieces as they kick into life. Fluids have formed. Hundreds of living chemicals develop as atoms are redeployed and recombine and flow and interact in each individual cell. Chemicals have combined with the fluids. Blood and lymph begins to circulate as life hits the heart pump saturating each one of those trillions of cells. Lungs activate and oxygen floods the entire structure. The electrical signaling systems comes alive. Father is rubbing his hands together in excitement, "I love it when a plan comes together." Jesus is looking on, thinking, "That's what I'm going to look like one day – hey, not bad, not bad at all." It has been a fearfully and wonderfully contrived piece of engineering. Development that takes twenty-five years to complete in us has been accelerated to just a few hours in the prototype.

The whole complex arrangement is throbbing and resonating with life. It's a goer.

Then –

Almighty God who has built the Milky Way and all the other billions of galaxies out there in Creation, kneels and breaths into the nostrils of the mud-man, his very own life and Spirit – his very own DNA – the very energy and life force that had produced all Creation.

Then –

The mud shape has been slowly changing colour and texture and now, features have come to life. He wriggles and sits up – opens his eyes – and gasps at what he sees. The first sight the human race ever saw was the majesty and blazing glory of Almighty God – Father and Son and Holy Spirit – all standing there in astonishment.

Because the Family is gazing in awe at this gloriously awesome creature they have just made. A reflection of themselves. This is what THEY look like. As they are, so is he. This magnificent man, the most beautiful being to have been created in all Eternity with the completeness and perfection of the life of the Creator of all Creation flooding through his veins – WOW. God is satisfied and pronounces the new man to be "very good." The pinnacle of Creation – the pinnacle of perfection. Well, until Eve shows up anyway.

A few weeks/months/years/decades later, God had realised that Adam was not performing to his maximum potential so he designed a booster for him. Eve was installed into Adam's life to be a super-charger for him and "showing up" as she did was setting the pattern that half the human race is designed to follow but which has been missed ever since. While Adam had been made from earthy clay, God made Eve from Adam. If you are God, you can do things like that. Father God's personal DNA breathed into Adam is the same as was infused into Eve. Adam and Eve were truly "one flesh". Eve was made to complete Adam. That's the way it works folks!

Do you know, that arrangement of bits and pieces God built into Adam, kept working for 930 years. A life span that long – in perspective, would take us back to the ancient history of "1066 And All That". (OK – that's a bit from English history – see Google).

Adam lived very close to 1,000 years and if he hadn't screwed up he would still be with us today. He was designed and built and intended to live forever. We humans are indeed "fearfully and wonderfully made" – and we are going to live for ever anyhow.

For you folk who have had drummed into you that you are an unplanned very inconsequential accident that just happened to randomly develop over several million eons – the history of Adam and his descendants is in Genesis chapter five. The whole chapter is the genealogy from Adam to Noah, the years they each lived – lots of years – their descendants – and there would have been many more than those named. It has been guessed that at the time of Noah's flood there could have been twenty million people on the Earth. The genealogy from Noah to Abraham is in chapters ten and eleven. I suggest you read the whole of Genesis in a Modern English Bible. Apart from it being fascinating history, it will undo a lot of woolly thinking about the beginning of things. The genealogy from Abraham to Jesus is in both Matthew and Luke in the New Testament. Check out a website named – "Akhlar: Timeline of Jewish History". It will take you through from Adam to their re-occupation of Israel in 1948 Adam is a historic person, not a myth or fable. Adam is your original grampa, and he is a big improvement on being a dollop of swamp goop.

When we are dealing with the historical beginning of things as set out in the Bible, we are not dealing with wild guesses and fantasy. Leave that to the experts who try so hard to convince themselves that there is no God. It doesn't work of course, but they keep trying. Many of the landmarks and locations given in the history of those early times is still there, You can visit Abraham's tomb. A lot of the locations referred to in the New Testament are still there.

OK – back to here and now – this is where you come in.

Built into every man and woman who ever lived on this planet is the capacity to live in the fullness of the life and character and holiness of our Creator. Made in the image of God Almighty. Filled with the abilities and capacities of God Almighty. There are no limits or restrictions built into this new creature. You are made to be, and are intended to be, a duplicate of your Maker.

At the same time it is healthy to recognise that us little humans simply don't have capacity to even imagine, let alone see or understand, the sheer Almightiness and hugeness of God. He made us in his image and likeness, but he is too big for us to probably **ever** really get to know. He has the capacity to have built several hundred billion galaxies – and lots of little atoms and electrons. We can't do that. We need to understand that he really is God Almighty. He really is Eternal Creator of everything. We must get hold of this. You church people – this is not a sermon you will forget before you finish lunch. Get hold of it. You don't know this and you should know this. Get hold of it. But we can know **HIM**. We can know his heart, We can know his love. Look what he did on Skull Hill outside Jerusalem away back then.

Everything that has anything to do with anything is hanging on the fact that God is God. Not our concept of God. Not our imagination of what God is. Not any kind of religious performance or paraphernalia. Not anything except that God is a person and you can know him and he wants you to know him and he has gone to a lot of trouble so you *can* know him and he wants you back to where he made you to be.

Creator God built we human men and women a class of being more advanced than anything he has ever previously made. We humans are a copy of God. Nothing has changed from his end of it. No other creature in existence has been made in the image and likeness of God Almighty except us. Not angels, not horses. Just we humans.

Look, if we could only see what he made us to be – oh my – but we would be a lot different than we are right now. God loves us so much. He loves us drastically. God's love for us and his intention for us is of such consequence it has him doing really weird things that make no sense to us. God and everything involving God is so massively complex and huge it is way beyond anything we can understand and even find hard to believe. Yet – we are made to be and are intended to be, full-blood sons and daughters of this Creator Lord God Most High. We are made to be the same status in the household as Son himself. Let's get hold of that.

CHAPTER THREE

MAKING THE CONNECTION

We were conceived in the heart of Father God before anything was. We are at the heart of everything God has done since before there was a beginning. That's why he made us and that's where we fit into his Grand Eternal Scheme Of Things – but look at what we have done to ourselves. We humans have allowed ourselves to sink into the mess we have made of ourselves all over the world, resulting in a situation on Planet Earth that defies credibility. It makes no sense at any level.

The thing I find so hard to understand is that before time began and eons before he ever made our first parents, God knew what was going to happen – but he did it anyway. Before the first human was made, God arranged that he would take a really drastic action to make it possible for us to be cleaned up and restored to being the Sons and Daughters of The Most High he originally intended. Yes he did – and that is one more evidence that the way God does things demonstrates we are kidding ourselves when we think we have him all worked out.

Why did God do that? What on Earth did he think he was he doing? He had plenty of time to change his mind about us – but he didn't. What was Eternal Creator really up to when he made us? By the time Adam was made, he had long ago been living in his home in Heaven. He had squillions of angels to keep him company. And just look at us!!! And now national establishments around the world spend serious resources trying to convince us he doesn't even exist. They are so scared of him they go to endless trouble to get this non-existent God out of their country.

Just look at what we humans, made in the image and likeness of God, have allowed ourselves to become. As a race, we have defied him. If any of us were God we would have written off the whole bunch of us a long time ago. But he didn't.

What could he see in us that made it worth his while for Jesus to submit himself to the atrocities inflicted on him at Jerusalem, just so we pathetic losers could be brought back to being the union of life with Father he built us to be? Why did he do it?

Take a look. That is Eternal Creator God Almighty skewered up there on that Italian gallows left hanging in the sun to die. Why? Being executed as a criminal. Why? On this Planet. Why? What is it he could see in us that drove him to do that?

There is a line in Hebrews 12 that says – "He, – Jesus – for the joy of obtaining the prize that was set before him, en-dured the cross, despising and ignoring the shame, and is now seated at the right hand of the throne of God."

We are the prize that enabled him to endure the brutality and humiliation of what he was living through on the cross –

because he could see you – and he was copping what was coming to you instead of you having to go through it yourself. You can say with Paul – "I am crucified with Christ." Not that you will be – but that you were. It is a done deal. It's over. That was you up there being punished for your sinning and affront to the holiness of God – except that it was Jesus there taking your place so you wouldn't have to. Yes – he loves you that much. Knowing he was taking your place filled him with joy unspeakable and full of glory. He loved you that much.

If only we could catch a glimpse of the esteem in which he holds us – of Father's intentions for us – of his intentions for you – of the magnitude of his own majesty he has built into you – of the love for you that has been the driving force in him since before time was – how different life would be. How different we would all be. We are not designed to be scrabbling around where we too often find ourselves. We are not wired to be messing with some of the stuff that tends to occupy so much time and attention. We do it anyway.

Yes, of course, there was Adam's "Fall". But do we really know about being "Lifted Back Up Again"? It would make such a difference if we did. That Jesus died on the cross, unscrewed everything Adam had screwed up. I don't know how he did it, but he did. That colossal clanger Adam managed to pull was not the end of everything. It did create problems, massive problems, but regardless of what those difficulties might be, nothing has changed of Father's intensions when he built that man in the garden.

We must have firmly locked into our gizzard that the fixed and unchangeable eternal point of it all is that God set out to fulfil his dream to have a family of sons and daughters, men and women – including you – who are the same species of being he is, and to this very day what he set in motion way back then remains right on target and we are part of it. We must get hold of that.

I have problems trying to even imagine, let alone describe, the impossible vastness and complexity of God and his Creation. This is our Dad we are talking about. The Bible tells us in several places that Jesus is the Creator of everything – out there and in here – and I find it very difficult to relate the Jesus I know to being the Creator of the unbelievable, incredible, brain frying massiveness of it all. And then to realise that this is the same Jesus who wants so much to be living his life in us. The Bible has a line "The life I now live in this flesh is Christ who lives in me," He is here to share himself with us and live in us and complete us. He became like us so we could become like him. This is so ridiculously impossible – but that's what he did – and is still doing.

I can see the possibility of confusion emerging as I talk about God, and then about Jesus, then about Holy Spirit and refer to each of them as God. These really are three separate "People" who can be seen individually – well, you really can't see Holy Spirit – and interacted with – and although we people are a copy of God – they aren't "people". Perhaps "Persons" would be better or "Supreme Beings". Just remember we were made to the same specifications as they are. But regardless of how we describe them – people I have personally known have been taken on visits to Heaven and they talk with Jesus, very occasionally with Father, and are able to interact with invisible Holy Spirit, who is the Power Force of the Godhead and of Creation. Sometimes Jesus, appearing as a man, has visited people on Earth whom I have personally known.

Just a note for the church people – particularly the clergy – who insist that God is one person with three attributes. It was not Father who was crucified. It was not Jesus who came to the upper room on the Day of Pentecost. It was not Holy Spirit who fed the five thousand men – plus women and children – with one boy's lunch. Reading the New Testament from time to time could be a good way for a lot of church people and their teachers et al – to spend a bit of time.

Holy Spirit lives here all the time and he is everywhere at the same time. When you are God you can do that.

Look, you will never understand God, so don't bother trying. God is three "persons" but they are a team of one. God is that team and each part of the team is God.

But then, look at you. You are made of three parts too. YOU – that is the *essential* person you are – you are a spirit just like God is and that part of you can never die. The *functional* you, the active component of your spirit is your soul, and that will never die either. Your soul is the source of your intellect, your emotions – your ability to think, to love.

Your soul transmits to the outside what is going on inside through the physical electrical and electronic computer circuitry of your brain. You don't love somebody with your brain. Love – and all those strong emotions and feelings that make you who you are originate deep down in the inner recesses of who you really are. And you know it. You probably know all about having a broken heart, but you have never heard of anyone having a broken brain. You are who you are deep down inside your innermost being.

When you see yourself in the mirror, what you are looking at is not you. What you can see there is the house you live in and the vehicle you get around in – *your mobile home*. And that mobile home is the most fantastically beautiful vehicle that only God could have come up with, It is so clever, that with a bit of help you can even make another one – or another dozen – like it. Think that through when you have a few spare weeks. How does it happen? Swamp goop? You know better.

The wonders we are involved with. The beauty of holiness flooding all around us is there, it is here, it is constant, it is the environment God has us living in. Regardless of the clutter that is also everywhere, we really can walk with God pretty much immune from the influences that are trying to get at us and screw us up.

And you know what? Most people don't want to know about it – but they do know – and so do you. That's why I am writing this. Whatever it is going on between you and God – you know. While folk are trying so hard to block God from interfering with their lifestyle, lying there wide awake at two o'clock in the morning, deep down you know that something vital is missing from your life. Especially you church people – and your clergy. That missing component is God. Let me say again, that church and religion and the Bible are not God. Very few church people – or their clergy – really know God.

People everywhere are starving for substance and reality, desperate for a real tangible relationship with God. They don't realise that the lifestyle they cling to so ferociously, all that football and beer, the movies, the church, the good works, the clubs and making money, is in fact their clawing desperation to get back to the Garden from which they had been expelled. Longing, yearning to talk with their Dad in the cool of the day. God-starved people all screaming inside for that broken fellowship to be restored. Deep, deep down we all really want to know God.

Well, it is God who has built that desperation in you. He is trying to get you back to where you belong. He wants you and he to enjoy each other's company. The same God who has set off that pressing urgency in you is right there where you can talk to him – right now. The disasters and calamities that have torn you apart did not come from him. He wants to hold you close and comfort you and let you know it will all be OK. Let his love soak into you. Tell him you want to know him. Just ask him. He's listening. He wants you back. He needs you back to being what he built you to be.

SO – LET'S FIX IT.

What people think or don't think, believe or don't believe, has nothing to do with it. The recorded historical fact is that God gave Adam a no-brainer and Adam blew it. His instructions were, "You can eat anything you like from all these thousands of fruit trees on these many square miles of orchard but here is one tree from which you are forbidden to eat. Just this one tree right here. You must not eat any fruit from this tree here in the middle of the garden. This is a serious matter, take it seriously, because the day you eat anything from **this** tree, **that** day you will surely die". The original word is die – die. The same word repeated. A very emphatic statement.

This situation, set up by God himself was far from being an act of pettiness or triviality. A new component has entered the equation and that component is **the holiness of God.**

This man has been equipped with that holiness. At the same time, the power to choose is also built into him. He is being given the opportunity, made possible from having that living holiness of God inside him, to develop the capacity of choice and as a result, make right decisions. And he has the advantage most of us don't get when we need to decide something. He was told precisely what course of action to take and the consequences that would occur if he made the wrong choice. The power to choose built into each of us carries a fearful responsibility.

The plain, recorded historic fact is that Adam did eat that fruit and he die-died. He had made a disastrous choice and had blown it. Really, really blown it.

But the history tells us he lived on for another more than nine hundred years. Do we have a contradiction here? Did God make a mistake? Was he exaggerating?

You become involved here, so read this bit carefully.

Adam did die the same day he deliberately disobeyed God. He lost his connection with Holy Spirit who had been implanted into him the day he was made. He lost his God-breathed-in holiness. Holy Spirit withdrew and was no longer resident in Adam. God will not even attempt to co-exist with rebellion and disobedience and unholiness at any level. Adam the man lived on. He fathered a large family. But the God-life that had made him complete was no longer there. He was now incomplete. He could no longer function as he was built to function. When Adam "knew" Eve and she conceived and gave birth to the children who became our ancestors, that was **after** Adam and Eve had taken that disastrous bite – and had lost it.

This could well be where you are at right now.

The state of incompleteness and lostness has been passed down through succeeding generations of people, right down to us. We are all *born* die-died. We need an infusion of God-life so we can be and can live as we were designed and intended to be and to live.

Stay with it.

What God set in motion in the garden is the way things were intended to be and at the end of the day that is how things are going to be. And we know it. In spite of the human race deciding we don't need God, we have been scrabbling to get back to the garden since the day we were expelled from it. We know. Virtually every society on Earth has set up some arrangement to help them get back in there. Some of them go about it in funny ways – but they know – we all know.

For you folk reading this who have never really come to a place of "knowing" that connection with God – this is what happens:

You know your body must have a continuing input of air and food and water as fuel for it to remain operational. OK, that is maintaining and servicing your mobile home and we both know we spend a great deal of time and effort attending to that mobile home. But the mobile home is not you.

You are the person, the spirit person, the life source, the **essential** you, the character and personality, who lives on the inside – and you communicate with the outside world through the operating system called your soul.

Your soul is the **functional** you, your emotions, mind, intellect, memories, imaginations, will, attitudes, inclinations, desires, hopes, dreams, skills, artistry, music – connecting the spirit and body.

Your soul communicates to the outside world what you are on the inside through the physical electronic computer circuitry of your brain. It is your soul that absorbs input, again, through the physical processor of your brain and develops attitudes and opinions and collects memories and likes and dislikes. That is happening in your soul, not your brain. Your brain is the receiver, the processor and connector and transmitter. Yes, you are really an extremely complex piece of automated equipment that requires continual scheduled maintenance.

OK, let's get into it.

You know your body is built to need continual intake of food and air and fluids to grow and develop and function, and you know your soul needs a continual intake of healthful nourishment for it to function correctly.

In the same way, your spirit is built to need connection with God.

It is like epoxy glue. It comes in two tubes, a white tube and a red tube. The material in either tube is quite useless alone. The same amount of paste from each tube must be thoroughly mixed and blended until it becomes a homogeneous compound that can't be separated. The adhesive from tube "A" must have the same amount of catalyst from tube "B" added and blended or the adhesive just remains a sticky mess. Neither of the two parts can function independently. Both need each other to be able to fulfil their destiny. It is the same with God and us. We are the adhesive, he is our Catalyst. We must be well-mixed in equal parts until we are a homogeneous entity. Adding God to our life completes us and makes us functional. And, adding God to our lives completes God too. He wants we and he to be that homogeneous entity. It's not a one-sided arrangement.

The real essential you is that spirit. It is who you are. It is your character and personality. You are designed and built in such a way that you cannot function properly, you are incomplete, you are "crippled" until you and God are reconnected and fused together with each other. *The real you – the essential person you are – needs to be joined to and blended together with God.* That is what completes you. You will be empty and unfulfilled – even a sticky mess – all your life until that happens.

OK – here is a "how to" that will help make it happen.

God has been trying to get your attention for a long time –
and now he has it. Holy Spirit is at work in you and has you
reading this, and right now he is bringing you to that point of
desperation where you are ready to call out to God and tell
him you can't keep living like this. The thing is, God built
you to be holy and unholiness in you is making you hard to
live with, and you have had enough.

You get quiet and alone with God. You know he is here and
you know his holiness is all around you. His holiness around
you and your unholiness in you – clash. Your whole being is
crying, please God, help me. God I need you. God I want you
to take over the running of my life.

You tell him out loud you are sorry for the life you have been
living. You tell God and yourself you want to make a complete turn-around from this point in your life.

You ask him to forgive you – then thank him that he has.

You ask him to come into your life and take over the running
of it – then thank him that he has.

There is a line in Acts 16 where Paul is in jail and he is telling
his prison guard, "Believe on the Lord Jesus Christ and you
will be saved." That word translated "believe" is – "take
yourself out of your own keeping and put yourself into the
keeping of another" – a decision to trust – a commitment –
in this case – to Jesus Christ. "Saved" in this verse means a
complete restoration of everything.

**Your commitment – your giving of yourself to God is as
deliberate and as intentional as your marriage commitment**

– only much more so. You have made the deliberate decision to spend the rest of your life with this person. This is the turning point. This is when Holy Spirit moves in and completes you. Your giving of yourself is absolute, total, complete, holding nothing back. You are in this for keeps – like for Eternity. That commitment makes you part of God's family and household.

So – you have deliberately, knowingly and willfully handed over yourself and the running of your life to God.

You will probably be aware at this point that "something has happened". The "clash" has probably dissolved. If not – keep at it until it does. It will happen. It may be impressed on you there is still something you need to fix – like forgiving someone. So fix it, and get on with it. We are dealing with Eternity.

You may find that in a day or two you suddenly think the whole thing was fantasy and that nothing has really changed. That often happens as the habits and forces you lived with for so long rebel at being evicted and want to come back home. Just thank Jesus again for what he has done and the intruders will leave. Do that as often as the attacks come until they get tired of it and go somewhere else.

That "something happening" is the new baby being born. You are being "born again". Religion is not involved. It is the connection being made between God and yourself that is completing you. God has moved into you and has blended his Spirit with your spirit as he fuses himself into your deep inner person making you to be one person with him. His holiness has replaced your unholiness. **You have become**

that homogenous entity. I think that is worth getting excited about.

Holy Spirit moving in and taking over IS the "new birth". It is the new start of a new life. All the good stuff this book is talking about is now yours to appropriate. Grow and develop into the level of life God has prepared for you and the enjoyment of it.

And to make this the real deal, you have also "passed from death to life"; you are going to live forever with God. AND – you will be welcomed as a son or daughter into God's family with all the rights and privileges attached.

Check what Paul said in 2nd Corinthians 5:17 to see what has actually happened. "If any person is engrafted in Christ, he is a new creation, a new creature altogether. The old, previous moral and spiritual condition has passed away. The fresh and new has come." I think that is worth getting excited about too.

Your sin was dealt with by Jesus on the cross. Since his crucifixion, sin has never been the problem. The problem is that people can't be bothered to appropriate – to receive for themselves – what Jesus achieved on the cross. It's that easy. It's the same as when your rich uncle died and left you a fortune but you never bothered to claim it and transfer the funds into your account. Sooner or later you will discover what happened when Jesus was crucified and you will dissolve when you realise he really loved you that much.

Now, I don't want to turn you off, but the New Testament talks a lot about church. But what the Bible is talking about and what is being passed off as church these days are the proverbial chalk and cheese. They have nothing in common and we will talk about that mess as little as possible.

But the new baby you have become needs family and friends around you right now. The situation is a bit like trying to get one piece of wood to burn. It doesn't work. But put two pieces together and they will burn all day. You need the "other piece". Pray – ask God to put you in contact with the people he has prepared to be your family. You will have to really trust God because there are a lot of religious people out there ready to screw you up. Avoid accepting an invitation to "come to church" with someone. Involvement with the existing religion industry can waste years of your life – sometimes – all of it. You really need a supernatural act of God at this time.

At its simplest, church is two people and God sitting around drinking coffee and talking with each other. God invented coffee. But what Jesus really set up was a group of people because the different abilities needed to make things work are given to different people. The New Testament talks about "the Body of Christ", the inference being that just as your own human body has all those many components all working together to get things done – that's the way church is supposed to work. Perhaps a bit more later, but the big issues are that God intends to achieve what he wants done through that group of people. Church is not buildings or rituals or programs or sitting on pews – **or** standing in pulpits. From this point, if I say "church", you read – "group of people"

What I am saying in the next few pages will probably bore the socks off some of you, but there are a lot of church attendees who are in an awful mess and this is for them. You can join in too. It could save you wasting a lot of years of your life. Messing with church can destroy you. Church actually inoculates you with very small doses of God that make you immune from ever catching him.

God designed church – your group of friends – so ordinary people can become extraordinary people. **Your group of friends God has connected you with exists to get you restored to his original intention of you being duplicates of Jesus.** Yes – that IS in the Bible.

People involved with "church" programs and rituals and traditions and doctrines, and clergy and general religious carry-on **know** what they are doing and believing is not working and are starving for reality and substance. They arrive home as frustrated and empty as they had left.

Genuinely "born again" men and women with Holy Spirit living inside know that Jesus did not submit himself to the horrors of the cross just so they can sit on a pew and be fed a very forgettable sermon every Sunday morning for the next fifty years. Sitting on a church pew is futility and frustration taken to its extreme.

The intended **result** from getting together with your group of friends – is that through the interaction of the many structural components making the Body of Christ functional, by working together with Holy Spirit and each other, ordinary people are transformed into becoming extraordinary people, duplicates of Jesus, the same as but more advanced than was Adam when God breathed himself into Adam's nostrils.

That's one reason we are so important to Father. He wants to see Jesus duplicated in you and throughout the human race just as he intended when he made Adam and we are not of much use to him until we get there. And in these desperate times he needs us there.

With Holy Spirit energising the structure made up of the assembled individual specifically functionally formed Body components, people change into becoming of 'the measure of the stature of the fullness of Christ' – duplicates of Jesus – and is the most exciting and almost unbelievable transformation – the caterpillar to butterfly miracle – of men and women and teenagers and children, that has happened to humans since Adam was made. Yes, it really is in the Bible.

CHAPTER FOUR

OUR AMAZING CREATOR

I began the search that resulted in this book – and a whole bunch of others – being written, more than fifty five years ago, and that was built on thirty years of solid Evangelical teaching and church absorption since infancy. I learned to talk saying Bible verses. I even knew what "whosoever" means. My mum had me reading the King James Bible when I was four. I grew up in a strong Open Brethren church in a town until I was fourteen, then the family moved to a dairy farm way up the coast, and that was the end of my formal education. But not the end of me learning stuff. I have never studied astronomy nor any of the sciences that relate to much of what I am saying here, but in my working life I was a very good mechanic and machinery designer-builder. By that I mean, my business was to know how things work, and if they are not working, find out why and fix it. That is – to observe and understand and resolve the situation – and I didn't get paid unless I got it right.

And that native capacity for observation has resulted in me being absolutely flabbergasted on many occasions observing the complexity of Creation, whether it was watching ants at work in my kitchen, or a baby being born, discovering more and more of the marvel of the unknowable complexity of engineering our bodies really are – and infinitely more so at the impossible complicatedness of our soul and spirit. Our ability to love and think and design and create and talk and sing and make music – and just looking at what is all around us – and out into the heavens on a bright moonless night. There are times when we just shrivel into nothingness as we find ourselves surrounded with marvels so amazing we are lost. Involvement with God is – well – exciting – and can even be scary.

Let's start small. Real small.

God invented zygotes. A zygote is a single human cell, who, at two microns, is around fifty times smaller than the diameter of one of your hairs which is around one hundred microns. Most normal cells are around one micron, the male spermatozoon is a half micron and the female ovum is around two microns. A micron is one thousanths of a millimetre or one millionth of a metre. There are twenty five millimetres to an inch.

You were once – actually, you still are – the most marvellous evidence of the beauty of the heart and mind – and brilliant cleverness – of our Creator God. For a few minutes as you were coming to life, you were a zygote. You weren't much of a big shot at that point. Anyone would need a very powerful microscope to even see you. Yet – at that point in your life, you were a full blown person standing in your stockinged feet at two / one thousandth – 2/1000th – of a millimetre – or at 2% of the diameter of one of your hairs. Yes you. But look at you now. How did that happen?

You were once your mother's egg cell who has just invited your dad's sperm cell in for coffee and an out-of-this-world-getting-to-know-you party is in full swing. These two are made for each other. In just moments, the twenty-three chromosomes – means: "personal specifications and construction detail", or even "barcode", your dad's spermatozoon has brought with him are reaching out and pairing off with the twenty-three chromosomes your mum's ovum had ready waiting for him, completing the complement of forty-six chromosomes required as your personal development blueprint. That combination of chromosomes contained the information and switching on capacities that activates everything that makes you to be you. You are unique in the entire world – and maybe in all the world since Adam and his wife began their family. Within just minutes, we are no longer dealing with sperms and egg cells – we are dealing with you – and you have become a brand new living person packaged in a bundle you need a pretty fancy microscope to even see. Mum's egg cell and dad's sperm cell have now fused into being one completed cell, not two. That newly completed cell is a zygote, and this zygote is the full-blown man or woman, spirit and soul and body you have grown to be. This invisible cell is you – a living person who is alive. You are all there. You are a complete human being. You are the most fantastically marvellous piece of creation in the universe. Yes, it's you we are talking about.

Be nice to zygotes. He/she could be a Billy Graham or Mother Teresa, a Wolfgang Mozart or Nikola Tesla. Just be nice to him/her.

A point to ponder for those who have had drummed into you since your schooldays that you are the result of some random accident in a swamp millions of years ago. The twenty three chromosomes in each of the male and female cells, which when joined, have formed the zygote having forty six chromosomes – are exactly the same make-up in every man and woman in the entire world from north to south and east to west, and which has been for 5773 years. Work out the odds of that being possible for billions of people for thousands of years. If a man from Hamerfest in Norway, the most northern town in the world and a woman from Ushuaia in Argentinean Patagonia, the most southern town in the world, had a baby – that baby would be exactly the same makeup as every other baby anywhere in the world. You are not the product of random chance – and neither is anyone else – except perhaps those mindless sub-species infesting "science" and education departments scattered around the world. Those pathetically deformed creatures didn't ought to be allowed to walk down the street unless holding the hand of an accompanying adult.

When God made our prototype parents in the garden so very long ago he built into them the ability to make more people like themselves. Think that through for a while – like about twenty years.

Creator God set up this arrangement so that what he built Adam to be on Planet Earth would continue to be down through the human race for as long as Earth remained. Six thousand years later the system is still working fine, but humans have made a real mess of it.

Creator God can build things so incredibly small we cant see them. Even with the most powerful microscopes, you cannot see an atom, and you most certainly cannot see the electrons and protons and quarks and energy components from which atoms are built. God is very clever. Scarily clever.

God is the Creator of everything you can see on Planet Earth and a whole heap you can't see, and he is the Creator of everything you can see in the night sky – and you can't see much of that either. Out in the country on the darkest night you can only see around five thousand stars. There are hundreds of billions of galaxies out there and you can't see even one of them. Not stars, not even constellations – but *galaxies*. Hundreds of billions of them.

In the original writing of this book I spent a whole chapter on the massive hugeness of Creation. This time I want to avoid distractions, so I will only leave in this next bit. But I do want to get across to you that what God designed and built you to be part of is a very great deal more than sitting around in Heaven for millions and billions of eons.

A while back, somebody sent me an email containing a link that opened up a whole new awe of Creation, and of the Creator. It was a series of illustrations comparing the size of Earth with other astronomical bodies in our Milky Way galaxy. (Google: "Our Earth in Perspective").

Earth in relation to the Sun, for instance, (not from Google) is as a single grain of wheat is to a full bag of wheat. Before the days of bulk handling, a "bag of wheat" was the international standard measurement for that product. It weighed 180 pounds (81kg) and contained three bushels – or twenty-four gallons – of grain. So, if you have twelve, two-gallon (10*l*) buckets filled with wheat, that represents the size of the sun.

Now, if you take out one single grain of wheat from one of those twelve buckets full, that single grain against the twelve buckets full, is what Earth looks like compared to the Sun. And that tiny speck of a planet we call "home" is then swung around the Sun, tied to an invisible string 93 million miles (150million km) long, at a speed of 60,000 miles (96k km) an hour.

It takes a whole year to do the circuit, and that is what changes our seasons. Well, actually, our year is the time it takes to make that circuit.

This is an enormous trip of nearly 600 million miles around a circular track 186 million miles (300 m. km) from side to side. We are also spinning like a top at 1,000 miles (1,600km) an hour at the Equator, and that gives us day and night. And we do this every day, every year!?!? There's no stopping us. I mean, we're really going places – real fast!

How on Earth did God do that? That trip and rotation has been running without even once stopping for an oil change since God fixed and re-set the affairs on Earth the week that culminated in Adam being made nearly 6000 years ago. No, I'm not saying its rotation and orbit began then, but like everything else on Earth at that time, things were badly out of kilter and the Creator fixed it that week – to the point that those timing sequences still operate with such precision they are calculated to the second.

But it was Betelgeuse on the last page of that "Earth in Perspective" illustration that caught my attention. I had read about this object many years earlier and had been impressed, but its statistics are really mind-blowing. There is another even bigger star on that page named Antares, but we seem to know more about Betelgeuse so we'll stay with it for this illustration.

This massive star is around 640 light years from Earth, one light year being the distance light travels in one year which is 5,865,696,000,000 miles. That means that if we could travel at the speed of light, it would take 640 years for us to get to Betelgeuse It is part of the Orion constellation in our Milky Way galaxy, **and Betelgeuse is eighteen million miles *greater in diameter* than is the orbit of the Earth around the Sun.** A tunnel through its middle from side to side would be more than 200 million miles (322m. km) long. That is, it is the distance from Earth to the Sun, then the same distance out the other side, plus the equivalent of 750 trips around the Equator added to that. Betelgeuse is an awful big piece of real estate. It is 14,000 times more brilliant than our Sun.

Our home galaxy – The Milky Way – is conjectured to be 100,000 light years from side to side and 16,000 light years deep in the middle and is thought to be in the form of a flying saucer. It is thought to contain 400,000,000,000 (400b) stars. Each of these stars would have a planetary system – as does our Sun star. Creator God does not muck around when he does something.

As our Earth is as a single grain of wheat in relation to the Sun being a whole bag of wheat, *compared to Betelgeuse, our Sun is a football, and Betelgeuse is the football stadium.*

On poor little Planet Earth, we scarcely exist.

The guess was that there are around 125 billion – 125,000,000,000 – *galaxies.* (Not sure how they counted them) Not stars or planets or constellations – but galaxies. That is something like 125,000,000,000 Milky Ways. Now, in addition to all that, are the new discoveries made in the past ten years by the Hubble Ultra Deep Field space exploration in the infrared field, beyond the range of the Hubble optical telescope and there could be as many as another 200 billion galaxies out there. One of the HUDF photos of Creation up to ten billion light years distant from Earth is the base of the front cover of this book. The deeper they probe, the more there is. Some astronomers think the number is infinite. And may I humbly suggest that Creator God Almighty was not out there making all that stuff just to fill in a bit of spare time. What God is really up to is *WAY* over our heads. Yes, yours too.

As objects in space go, Earth would have to be among the most insignificant in existence. Yet the history of the whole human saga has God Almighty, Eternal Creator of all Creation showing up here on this micro-mini mud-ball and setting in motion a situation that defies credibility. Eternal Creator, God Almighty made human people on this miniscule Planet Earth. That in itself is beyond comprehension. But to follow the history and watch what humans have sunk themselves into being, then to have God Almighty allowing himself to be executed here on this mini-planet by these same people he had made, just so we humans could be restored back to being what was originally intended – is beyond human ability to even pretend to understand. What's going on????

OK – I am slowly building up to something, but first let us get you together with that group of friends God has prepared to be your companions. You and your friends have within you the capacity to turn the world right-way-up – and that is why you and the friends God has given you have been brought together.

You have been brought together by Holy Spirit so that the environment can be created where he knows he is welcome and he can come to your gathering and infuse himself into you and develop in you what is nothing less than you being made to be a duplicate of Jesus. That basically is the point of the existence of church. It is the 'mechanism' that enables our development to that standard in the group of friends Holy Spirit has connected you with.

God has set a program in motion and he has involved us. He has involved you. That's why he made us. But to be of any use to him we need to have allowed him to develop us into having attained a level of maturity and responsibility that amounts to us arriving at being nothing less than the standard of life Jesus himself is – "the measure of the stature of the fullness of Christ." Which is what Paul told his friends at Ephesus in Greece a long time ago. Nothing has changed. To those of you not having had much exposure to the Bible, a man named Paul wrote most of what is referred to as "epistles" – means letters – in the New Testament to his friends and congregations in Greece. Corinth, Galatia,(a province) Ephesus, Philippi, Colosse and Thessalonica were cities in Greece.

It could be a good idea to get yourself a New Testament in modern English. Something like "Good News For Modern Man," There is some fascinating history there, as well as some of the important things that will help you get a handle on what is going on. But I say again – what you really need to know will come to you directly from Holy Spirit himself.

Your group of friends and you are what is referred to in the New Testament as an "assembly" or "church".

Now, let's bring in that missing element I hinted at in the earlier part of this material – and that is the Person of Holy Spirit himself.

Holy Spirit is the missing component of virtually every gathering – in fact – everything that exists in the Western world.

When those letters that ended up in the New Testament were being written, Holy Spirit was a very real active part of everything that was going on and the people involved were still fresh and filled with his fullness.

Paul was telling the people at Ephesus that God has given them men to help the new people develop to the point of being "perfected and fully equipped" so they could do things themselves. **What these men brought to that gathering was Holy Spirit** – NOT preaching or teaching or "how to's". Information does not produce "perfected and fully equipped" people. Holy Spirit does. These men were able to transfer and impart Holy Spirit into the people gathering there and so produce the "perfecting and full equipping" needed to bring "the saints" – means – "people set apart" – in this case to God. We are all called to be saints. No, you don't get halos. The saints are just the ordinary people. These had already been given that Holy Spirit impartation enabling the standard of development where they were able to do the kind of things Paul told us was happening at Corinth – and probably was happening in all the churches. Check out what was happening at Corinth in his first letter to his friends there, chapter 12.

There were no pews or pulpits or clergy or laity in the early church. It was a group of people with many abilities present and active – some with pretty extra-ordinary abilities.

At that time when things were still fresh and new, it was normal for the men God had given to be able to impart Holy Spirit to people. It is still possible at this time, but the genuine article is very rare. So rare that until God makes his move preparing to launch his Kingdom it is not likely you will be coming into contact with each other. Since early last century there have been short-lived renewals of the release of Holy Spirit, but generally, all we have now is good intentions and wild promises that don't happen. The substance and reality of Holy Spirit activity in the Western world right now virtually doesn't exist. In the Western world right now, "The Body of Christ" does not exist at all – not even virtually.

SO – the new gathering I am talking about is people who have set themselves to get back to the reality of Holy Spirit interaction that was happening in those early days. Holy Spirit hasn't gone anywhere. He is very patiently waiting for us to get our act together.

The initial purpose and intention of that group of people getting together is that – as the first requirement – as being where you start – is you providing the environment that invites Holy Spirit to come to you and infuse himself into you, so you are able to develop until you become duplicates of Jesus.

So, let's get this show on the road.

Stage 1. you have committed yourself to Jesus with a giving of yourself as totally absolute as your marriage commitment.

Stage 2. you are together with the group of friends God has given you.

Stage 3 is where it starts to hurt. You get rid of all your ambitions and agendas and goals and programs. What God is about to do in you will be what he needs to have in you, so you and he can work together to get the job done. His way of doing things is very different to our way.

Stage 4. is the starting point of everything that God expects from his people, and we are of no use to him until we get there. You are in the position and condition now where, because Holy Spirit is at work in you and your friends, he is able to bring you to "mature adulthood; the completeness of personality which is nothing less than having attained to the measure of the stature of the fullness of Christ and the completeness found in him" that enables this to happen. That is where you start.

I know that at this time in history, something of very real consequence will need to happen to make this possible. I believe God is putting that part together right now. For instance, he has me writing this now at this time and you are reading it right now. But while we are waiting, there can be no place for presuming or pretending or doing things 'by faith' or 'let's see what God will do'.

The gathering of your group is specifically intended to produce that duplication of Jesus in you. How that will happen now is a whole nuther ball-game, but the required end result will be the same. Trust Holy Spirit to bring it together and make it happen. Holy Spirit is a very powerful Person, and if the right environment is prepared for him and he meets no obstructions he can get a lot done in a very short time. But until that transformation happens, nothing has happened and trying to make it happen can kill the whole thing.

Just the fact that you and your friends are deliberately getting together with the intention you are going all the way and you are sticking with it until it happens, could be making you the most consequential group of people on the planet. You are creating the environment where Holy Spirit knows he is welcome.

Let me spoil things for a moment. Even this must be put together by Holy Spirit. You can't read up some of the histories of "moves of God" – choose one – and start doing what these people did. All you and your friends can do is to let go your stuff and adjust your heart to the point where Holy Spirit can take you seriously. At this time in human history, I believe Holy Spirit is running around the world frustrated out of his socks, looking for the group of people we are talking about here.

THEN – when he finds you "something will happen" – as it inevitable will as God sets in motion what he has been building up to for a long time.

When Holy Spirit arrived in that "upper room" in Jerusalem that Pentecost Sunday morning, things took off quite dramatically. Yes – there had been a build-up of expectation as those hundred and twenty men and women waited ten days for that moment – and standing way back at this time and looking into the core of things – this was the critical turning point in The Grand Eternal Scheme Of Things clicking into place. It has never happened like that before or since.

CHAPTER FIVE

THE TIDE TURNS

The human mess did not catch God by surprise. He knew exactly what would happen even before the beginning of anything. God can be scary sometimes.

It continues to flabbergast me that he has done what he did just to enable us pathetic humans to get back to himself. It is beyond credibility that Creator God actually submitted himself to being crucified so we can be restored to full family status with him. To me, this is infinitely more mind boggling than anything in Creation – either out there or in here. It's waaaaay over our heads but that's what happened.

We must understand that God Almighty planned and **intended** that man should rule and reign on this planet. Adam was to get experience under his belt (OK – what belt, I hear you ask) and get in some practice at governing large constituencies, however, that intention came unstuck.

In the coming unstuck, it seems there could have been something going on there that was more than simple disobedience.

In a letter to his young friend Timothy, Paul told him that although Eve had been deceived, Adam was not deceived. Adam knew that Eve had already committed the act of disobedience that God said would kill them. Is it just possible that Adam's love for Eve was such that he chose to accept God's judgment with her rather than be separated from her? That he chose Eve above God?

Whatever the motive, **by participating with Eve in an act of deliberate disobedience, he handed his God-given authority and dominion over to Lucifer. That really was an act of serious high treason.**

And don't get too cocky or judgmental, you've been doing it your way all your life.

Serious as it was, Adam's disobedience did not in any way alter what God intends for the Earth or for the people he had made. God still sees things as he had planned in the beginning. He has not changed his mind, nor given up his dream.

The exciting thing is that now, since Calvary, all has been rectified and fixed. **Jesus did back up what Adam had undone.**

Jesus – referred to in the New Testament as "the Second Adam"- took back from the devil what the devil had hijacked the first Adam into giving him.

People can now be restored to the original intention of being duplicates of Jesus – but I don't know **anyone** who actually believes it. Church people reading the Bible can be very selective about what they choose to believe. Very few of them could fill two pages with what they believe the Bible says.

Most could never fill one page. They do their duty by God and put their put their Heavenly Fire Insurance premium in the bucket every Sunday morning That goes double for those who believe every word of the Bible from cover to cover. Very few church people have ever even read it from cover to cover.

The substance of what Jesus achieved while he was hanging on that cross is at the heart of Eternity and of Father God's eternal intentions for the human race. Eternity and all creation hinges on what was done there.

We can only guess at what happened and I know I have already said this, but this is the most important event to have happened on Earth or in Heaven or in all Creation, in time or all Eternity.

Here is this Being – Eternal Creator – who, for unimaginable billions of eons has been the One whose inconceivable might and force and power had released the flood of creative and constructive energy from within himself – who had built the Milky Way – and hundreds of billions of other galaxies besides – and those impossible zygotes – and atoms.

And here he is – having been flogged to within an inch of his life by the man creatures he had made – his back ripped open – stark naked – the weight of his body dragging on iron spikes hammered through his hands and feet – skewered up there on that Italian gallows and left hanging in the sun to die by the very same men he had made to be duplicates of himself – while a whole platoon of warrior angels with drawn swords are circling the area waiting for the command to attack – but it was never given.

We CAN know, that on top of all that, during those three

hours of darkness from mid-day till 3 o'clock that Friday afternoon, Jesus had infused into his person every sin and disobedience and iniquity and rebellion and blasphemy that ever was or ever would be committed – from Eve's first bite through to the last rebellious act committed by the last person alive on this planet – and Jesus was called on to absorb into himself the accumulated pent up wrath of God against this affront to their Creator by the human race who has deliberately chosen to live in sin and rebellion and disobedience.

I wonder if Jesus had realised what a devastating effect sin would have on the lives of people and domestic and national and global affairs when he had made that commitment way back before the foundation of the cosmos. And now this Creator-God-made-a-man was being called on to wear ALL that in himself while at the same time enduring his own personal physical agony of brutal execution by crucifixion.

No wonder the prophets saw him as grotesque, repulsive, not even appearing to be human. No wonder he cried out as he was even abandoned by his Father. We don't know. Maybe, we will never know.

But we DO know that as the result of all that happened there, atonement – means: "compensation/satisfaction" – was made, redemption – means: "buy back/recover" – was paid, reconciliation had occurred, and let's not kid ourselves, we have no idea what went on there. It was between Jesus and Father. It was by God for God. It was a political maneuver brought to completion in the Heavens and we will probably never know how that was done either.

But we DO know this too. When what he had set out to accomplish had been accomplished, Jesus shouted from the cross with a loud and triumphant voice:

"It is completely completed."

Whatever it was that had been done there it had achieved what was intended – and had been intended since even before the foundation of the cosmos world.

By a process of alchemy we have no capacity to understand, the blood Jesus had just allowed to be released from his human body through the atrocities inflicted on him by his executioners, has the power to blot out the sins we had committed, leaving us as though we had never sinned. And if that was not enough, by a process of transfer and identification, we were actually absorbed into Jesus while he was on the cross, to the extent that everything going on in him was also going on in us.

"I am crucified with Christ." says Paul.

That is not poetry. That is the fact of what happened there.

When Jesus died – you died.

And the whole process can be developed from that point, reaching right through to – **"the life I now live in this flesh is Christ who lives in me"** culminating in **"as he is – so are we in this world"**.

It is the matter of this identification with Jesus that enables us to enter into the actual ultimate **"measure of the stature of the fullness of Christ and the completeness found in him"**.

CONNECTING **GOD** AND **YOU**

But there is more. It is recorded in Hebrews 2, that through his death, Jesus 'destroyed him who had the power of death, that is the devil'.

Quite simply, what the devil had tricked Adam into giving up had been taken back from the devil by Jesus.

Authority was now back in the hands of the original owner of it.

The devil is no longer in charge.

By the transfer of that original authority back to us – Father's family- that's us – are once again the governing body.

What happened on the cross was a very great deal more than us merely having our sins dealt with so we could all go to Heaven when we die.

There was tremendous drama following the Cross. I have heard and read so many scientific and religious explanations of what caused the death of Jesus. From ruptures to a broken heart, loss of blood, shock, and a whole lot more. It was none of that. People seem to have forgotten that Jesus said that no man could take his life from him.

Instead, invigorated by what had been accomplished **he simply dismissed his Spirit** and his body slumped. But there are still some loose ends to tie up.

From the cross, directly and immediately he dived into Lucifer's bastion where the party to end all parties was in full flight. They've **got him**.

Imagine the horror in that place when Jesus suddenly showed up and scuttled **that** party.

He had been waiting for this moment a long time.

Jesus strode up to Lucifer – grabbed him by his scrawny neck – swung him upside down – and shook. Out of the imposter's pockets fell the crowns and scepters and symbols of national authority he had purloined over the centuries.

Jesus scooped up these objects – stashed them in his own pockets – (metaphorically speaking) – and with a mighty heave sent that monster howling down the corridors of the damned.

When Jesus died, the authority of the devil was destroyed.

After a couple of days trashing the joint and rendering it – and its inhabitants – useless, Jesus gathered his own people from the back galleries where they had been waiting for this day for hundreds and thousands of years and went outside.

Suddenly, Jesus found himself in total darkness and suffocating. There is near panic as a massive pressure is squeezing in on every particle of his body.

Not one – not even one – of his friends and disciples had believed a word Jesus had said about him coming back to life after he had died. They had all run away and hidden, while Joseph of Arimathea and Nicodemus actually made an attempt to embalm his body. The women who came to the tomb with their spices early that Sunday morning were there to complete the embalming of his face which Joseph and Nicodemus had left for them – or had run out of time on Friday afternoon with a special Sabbath looming.

That linen cloth plastered with all those spices – 100 pounds weight of it as John told us – so lovingly wrapped around his body by his friends on Friday afternoon, had shrunk and the compound had hardened like a concrete casing and he could neither move nor breathe.

At that instant, a rumbling as the stone is rolled back from the front of the tomb. The cloth is lifted from his face and there is Holy Spirit just visible in the early morning light. "Come out of that thing." – and Jesus found himself standing by the crypt dug from solid rock where he had just been lying – and took a deep breath. The cocoon can be seen, still holding the shape of his body. (There ain't no Shroud of Turin) A set of clothes is given him, and he dresses. Every movement hurts. He is hurting all over.

The events of last Friday come flooding back. Joy takes over. He has done it. It really is completely completed. It had all been worth it. He becomes aware that the prisoners he had released from Hades were standing there watching all this and waiting. Jesus handed this massive company over to Holy Spirit and told him, "Take these on to Headquarters, there are a couple of things I need to do. I'll meet you there shortly."

He stepped out into the dawn light and a woman is standing there – crying.

"Mary"

"Raboni"

CHAPTER SIX

THE PLAN IS TAKING SHAPE

Another party has been coming together, this time at Headquarters. Everyone is decked in full regalia. But right now, things have become very quiet.

Jesus has just arrived.

There is a gasp of shock. Apart from his security detail and Gabriel and some of the special angel troops who had been on duty roster in Palestine on Planet Earth at that time, no one had ever seen him like this. The last time they had seen Son his radiant glory had lit up the place. Now he is a drab and injured little human man having trouble walking. This was not the homecoming they were expecting. Very few there had seen him as a man. They had difficulty realising this was indeed Son.

He enters – pauses – human eyes adjusting to the brilliance of Heaven's glory. Now that he is actually here – possibly even a flash of doubt. Was what he had done last Friday REALLY been enough to blot out sin and the penalty of sin for the entire human race? Had it REALLY been completely completed? Had he REALLY pulled it off? It's crunch time.

Carrying the bowl containing the blood his escort angels had collected and have now handed to him, on badly injured feet he begins the most solemnly momentous walk ever taken in all Time and all Eternity, slowly, hesitantly, to where Father is seated on The Throne waiting, and places the bowl containing his blood at Father's feet. "I have done all you asked of me. I present my blood I have given to blot out man's sin and enable his reconciliation with you. Is this sufficient? May our people go free now?" Then steps back, head bowed, and waits for the verdict.

For half an hour there is a silence in Heaven that can be cut with a knife. The issues being resolved are the most consequential in all Eternity. This may even have been the dividing line between Eternity past and Eternity future.

Satisfied – all considerations carefully weighed up – Father looks across to Holy Spirit – grins and nods – then yells – **"it is done – it is sufficient – the people may go free."**

And Heaven erupts. Earth garments removed. Glory robes cover him, and hoisted on the shoulders of highest-ranking archangels Jesus is paraded around the courts of Heaven.

When things have quietened somewhat a full Solemn Conclave assembles. Jesus is promoted to Position and Rank beyond anything previously known. Absolute – Unlimited – ALL power – ALL authority – ALL dominion – in Heaven and on Earth and under the Earth is assigned to him. He is given **a name above every name.** He is "Lord of lords and King of kings".

He is so vastly different now to when he had entered. His appearance has changed. He is not even the same as the inhabitants of Heaven had previously known him. He has been restored to his regular physical size, normal for this sphere, and although the scars of those crucifixion wounds remain to this day, the radiance of earlier times is multiplied to a blazing glory never seen before.

The party really cuts loose.

(There has been teaching in circulation for several decades saying that in Heaven, Jesus is still a man and still a Jew. He is not. In the Heavens he can be composed of fire and assume the size of a mountain. In Heaven he is God Almighty together with Father and Holy Spirit.)

The festivities have ended. After having made a couple of quick commutes back to Planet Earth to reassure his friends and prepare them for the next development, Jesus is with Father and Holy Spirit in private quarters planning future strategies. The staggering implications of what had been accomplished are discussed, and now, what had been planned before the Cosmos had been formed, is to be resumed.

Reconciliation is absolute. We are right back to where we started.

It is up to us whether we take advantage of what happened there.

The grace and mercy and fixed intention of God is hard to work out. He must have wanted us awful bad.

It had already been arranged that Holy Spirit would take up residence on Earth, and beginning with the team Jesus had prepared, continue the work Jesus had begun. Holy Spirit would provide the wisdom and power, and working together with the disciples, the job would be done.

The intention is world conquest.

Nothing less.

Getting the planet back to where it had been intended from the beginning.

Now it can happen.

Before returning to Headquarters, Jesus had told his disciples what to expect As usual, it went clear over the top of their heads. But he had made his intentions clear. To let people know what had happened and the implications of that – and to bring to nations the restoration of righteous government under God to the point where it would actually happen.

After having seen him alive following the crucifixion, they did seem to have turned a corner. One hundred and twenty of them obeyed by staying put in one place for ten days – even if they did hold a business meeting and elected an officer. But Jesus had instructed.

"Don't attempt anything until you have been Equipped From On High. You will receive power when Holy Spirit has come upon you. You will do even greater things than I did. You are my especially assembled full blood brothers and sisters. You are our personal family – and you shall assault the fortresses of hell, and they will not be able to stop you."

Holy Spirit arrived right on cue and Pentecost happened. Now it was possible for all that Jesus had instructed to begin to happen.

But, as it turned out and as it has continued to turn out ever since, the baby Church got bogged down in local issues. The history of the Church Luke has given tells us that the team Jesus had prepared to take over the world and which Holy Spirit had empowered so it could happen – instead – actually set up a soup kitchen in the back streets of Jerusalem and began to receive offerings. That is NOT what Jesus had told them to do. He had actually told those fellows they could do greater things than he had been doing. Peter could have borrowed a hamburger from some kid there and fed the whole neighbourhood for weeks and have picked up fifteen baskets of fragments. He didn't need to take offerings.

Consequently, the big thing that Jesus commissioned them to do didn't even get started. It hadn't registered. It didn't happen and has never happened since.

It is history of course that most of the original team did eventually travel to other countries. The impact in each place varied. No nations became discipled, and most of the team came to a sticky end. In Armenia for instance, because the king's brother had become a Christian, Bartholomew was skinned alive then crucified upside down. It seems only John died of natural causes, but even that was after an attempt had been made to boil him in oil, but he didn't cook. He lived to be close to one hundred years of age.

Back at Jerusalem, it was Steven's murder – by the God worshipping, Bible teaching religion professionals – that got the people out of town and to where they were supposed to be and so began the spread of Christianity. Not from the apostles and prophets, they stayed in Jerusalem, but from the "common people".

Severe persecution had broken out and the Christians who "were scattered abroad went about through the land from place to place preaching the glad tidings." One version says. "Gossiping the gospel."

Ok – let's move up to the point in history where we live.

The unimaginable force of creative power resident in God Almighty released into his people by Holy Spirit at Pentecost has never been withdrawn. But down through the centuries, the church's inability and/or unwillingness to walk in unity of being with Father and Jesus and Holy Spirit as their daily lifestyle and to exercise that power resident in them – was pretty much universal. It was not called the "dark ages" without reason. Religion makes you feel warm and fuzzy. Holy Spirit doesn't.

Over recent centuries there have been flashes of evidence that the force is still with us and today there are ministries in some "developing" countries, who are seeing spectacular results from the exercise of that power. I have read that some are seeing dead people come back to life as almost routine. And why not. We were told we could do that.

In the Western church, there is a lot of expensive activity but not much to show for it and a lot of that is because of the mixture of world stuff pollution and business promotion techniques and religious codswallop and pretence and programs and agendas and personal impurity prevalent in our modern churches. Much, if not most, of what is done in church has little to do with God.

Quite frankly, God can't work in an environment such as is prevalent in the current Western church and if you look closely you can see that huge, elaborate, very expensive, ultimately useless religion industry is already beginning to crumble.

We were chosen in Christ before the foundation of the world, by God himself, that **we should be holy and blameless before him.** We **should** develop into that standard. We are intended to. It is not an option.

However, you don't see much of that. It's not happening.

There is a reason.

The awful truth is that what we have called "church" has no more relationship to what God intended the church to be than has your average pub bar. Both give a level of companionship, although the pub would win hands down on that score. Staring at the back of somebody's neck for an hour and a half is not fellowship. "Assembling yourselves together" is not lining up on a pew that is bolted to the floor and listening to some turkey in a pulpit waffling on about stuff about which he/she knows nothing.

Church is intended to produce an end result. If that end result is not showing up, something is not happening that is supposed to be happening.

In a former life I designed and built machinery, all kinds of things, but my bread and butter was sugar cane farming equipment.

When designing a machine, you start by knowing what the end product is to be and the raw material from which that end product will be formed. You confirm the power source. The point and purpose of the existence of the machine is that the energy provided by the power source enables the processes of the logical sequence of the machinery component function to occur and create an action which will transform the raw material into the desired end product. Most machines are fairly simple things. It is just that some employ more logical sequence than others.

Machinery does not consist of one Big Wheel.

Without calling the church a machine, it is never-the-less a device designed by the Ultimate Designer to produce an end result.

What I am saying is that Holy Spirit is the power source. The raw material is the men and women coming into the assembly. The functional components are the mature and already perfected and equipped duplicate-of-Jesus men and women ministering together in logical sequence to produce the end product. The end product is more duplicates of Jesus.

If that is not happening, then nothing is happening and if nothing is happening, nothing can happen. And that is exactly the situation church and the world is in at this time. It must be done God's way, or nothing is going to work. Look around you.

Paul's illustration is of a human body with all those bits and pieces "fitly joined together" and cooperating to produce a result.

Or a building. All those bricks and pieces of timber are cluttering up the work site until they are assigned their place and function. Until there is functional design and structure and components working together to produce a result, nothing has happened and nothing can happen. And may I observe that the foundation that holds the whole thing together is positioned right at the bottom of the pile, often deep underground and out of sight. The foundation is not sitting on top of the roof.

Why hasn't "church" been able to see that?????

The very best of what we are calling "church" these days is little more than a baby factory, or a recovery and maintenance operation. There is not even pretence of development. Nobody seems to know there is supposed to be development. Church emphasis is on about everything you can imagine, especially getting more babies born, then stashing them in the downstairs nursery for the rest of their life, anything, everything – except producing what Jesus built the church to produce.

CHAPTER SEVEN

WE ARE NOT HERE
TO PLAY GAMES

I get a bit serious in this chapter, Most of what I say here was originally written with church people in mind, but I invite you to join in. The big thing I am trying to get across is that if you had any idea who you really are, if you had any idea what you really are, your world, your country, your neighbourhood – you – things would be so very different where you are living right now.

The root of the problem is that from the day our parents pulled that awful clanger in the garden, and which continued until Pentecost, God had withdrawn himself from being the life inside Adam and Eve – and subsequently their descendents – and was always out in some place separate from the people.

God built us to be and he intended we would be, one person with him and that intention has been a force since before there was a beginning – and that's just the way it is. He intended he would be the life inside us. But when Adam knowingly and deliberately disobeyed – he actually defied God – God withdrew and left him to his own devices – and we inherited being left to our own devices. It is not the way he wanted it but that is the way it had to be. No matter who anyone was or what they did, God was outside them. Right up to the crucifixion, God and people were separate entities.

That situation has been fixed – but very few church people know it.

If you have been "born again" and have deliberately taken yourself out of your own keeping and even more deliberately have placed yourself into God's keeping, the fact is that God is now living his life **inside you**. An awareness of this can take us a long way past where most church folk spend their days.

The fact is that when Jesus came to Planet Earth, he was God who had become a man. He was as human as you are. He was stuck with being human. He had no advantage over you. For thirty years he had lived as an ordinary man facing every situation and temptation every man faces during his first thirty years. But, by his own deliberate choice of life-style, and having been tempted with, and overcome, every temptation you have been subjected to, he demonstrated it is possible for a human man to live his life in our world and not sin.

Then he had received that mighty infusion of Holy Spirit as John baptised him – exactly the same as you are able to receive. Because Jesus did not sin as other men sinned he was qualified to take an action that made the rest of us to be as though we had never sinned giving us the same status before Father God as he enjoyed.

In essence, he became like us so we could become like him.

I mean, not only were the sins we had committed blotted out, but our capacity and inclination to sin was also blotted out. That's what "I am crucified with Christ" means. From that point, for us to commit sin had to be a knowingly wilfully, deliberately rebellious act, and that is not a smart idea.

What Jesus came to do had been finished – actually "completely completed" or even "perfectly perfected" – so he went back to Headquarters. But before leaving, he made a double-pronged arrangement that would enable his people to actually attain to that standard of being that God Almighty had planned and designed from before the beginning.

Jesus arranged for his people on Planet Earth to have – 1 – his Holy Spirit and 2 – his gathered people as the combined means to produce the development required in them.

When Jesus established his Assembly it was intended to fulfil several functions.

First it was consolidating the re-connection between you and God.

As the church matured, that is followed by the process that produced the transformation of ordinary men and women into becoming a super race of creatures who were of the image and likeness of Creator God – duplicates of Jesus. This is the original intention of Father God. He built us to be as he is and to be part of his family with whom he could interact as being his equals. That's how he made us to be.

Back on Planet Earth, not much can happen until God has these Holy Spirit developed men and women as the foundation of all he has purposed.

Then – as being His "Body of Christ" – his people are able **to be functional representation of God Almighty on Earth.**

Then – **it was to combat and defeat the forces of darkness** who have successfully set in motion their program to create utter chaos on Planet Earth at this time.

Then – they were to **disciple the nations** on Earth and to bring them under the Government of God Almighty.

That is what Church is intended to be and do.

It didn't happen.

Being developed into attaining to the measure of the stature of the fullness of Christ and being duplicates of Jesus, is the end product church is designed to, and is intended to, produce, and is the foundation that MUST be laid if we are ever going to see God's Kingdom in operation on Planet Earth.

And that is where we start. It is not possible for anything to result until God has those duplicates of himself. People trying to do things through techniques and programs and with the best of good intentions, cannot produce anything except confusion and frustration.

It is Holy Spirit of God Almighty who is working together with the team and it is he who actually brings about the changes that result in producing duplication of the Person and character and abilities of Jesus in people.

I'll expand on that shortly, but for the moment, let's back track. Let's establish what we are talking about when we quote: "the measure of the stature of the fullness of Christ", or to use my term, "duplicates of Jesus".

This Jesus we are to duplicate – to whose stature we attain. This is the opening lines of Hebrews, "God has spoken to us in the Person of a Son whom He appointed Heir and Lawful Owner of all things, also by and through Whom He created the worlds and the reaches of space and the ages of time. He made, produced, built, operated and arranged them in order.

"He is the sole expression of the glory of God, the Light-Being, the out-raying or radiance of the divine. He is the perfect imprint and very image of God's nature (*this next bit is exclusive to Jesus*) upholding and maintaining and guiding and propelling the universe by His mighty word of power.

"When He had by offering Himself accomplished our cleansing of sins and riddance of guilt – (*now we can join in again*) – "He sat down at the right hand of the divine Majesty on high, taking a place and rank by which He Himself became as much superior to angels as the glorious Name and title which he has inherited is different from and more excellent than theirs."

So – what does "in Our image and after Our likeness" mean now?

What does "being seated with him in Heavenly places" mean?

What about the "Creator" bit?

How about "**as he** *is* **– so are we in this world**"?

Let's go further. From Colossians 1. "He (Jesus) is the exact likeness of the unseen God – the visible representation of the invisible. He is the Firstborn of all creation. For it was in Him that all things were created, in Heaven and on Earth – things seen and things unseen whether thrones, dominions, rulers or authorities, all things were created and exist through Him, and in and for Him.

"And He Himself existed before all things, and in Him all things consist, cohere and are held together. He also is the Head of His body, the church, seeing He is the beginning, the Firstborn from among the dead, so that He alone in every respect might occupy the chief place, stand first, and be pre-eminent. For it pleased the Father that all the divine fullness – the sum total of the divine perfection, powers and attributes – should dwell in Him permanently.

"And God purposed that through and by the service – the intervention of Him, the Son – **all things should be completely reconciled back to Himself – whether on Earth or in Heaven**, as through Him, the Father made peace by means of the blood of the cross."

Now – the parts of these statements referring to his eternal and creative being, and to his death and resurrection and restoration work – can only apply to Jesus.

All the rest of it is built into us. All of it.

This is the standard of being and accomplishment God intended when he built our prototype Adam.

This is the Christ – the Jesus – to whose standard we attain.

This is the measure of the stature of the Being we are intended to develop into being.

The ministration within the people gathered gets us started – but we grow from there.

We move to the place where we are able to say "**the life I now live in this flesh is Christ who lives in me.**" Our wonder as the awesome awareness of this fact explodes within us can make us hard to live with for a while. And when we realise we are actually jointly seated with him in the decision-making, strategy-planning Council Chambers of Heaven we are overcome with awe. We in this world are the same state of being as is Jesus in the Throne Room at Headquarters.

The thing I find so really incredible is that God has maintained his interest in this Planet at all. I am still wholly unable to understand the magnitude of what is going on here. It's massive, and I know that what I am seeing is scarcely scratching the surface of what is actually being set up. Not only would this planet itself have to be one of the most insignificant pieces of real estate in all Creation, but we humans became such a bunch of rebellious idiots I don't know how God puts up with us. But he does. He has set things in motion and he has chosen this tiny mud ball and the rebellious idiots on it, from which and through whom to spread his glory throughout all Creation.

It is impossible to get past the fact that Jesus – Eternal Creator God – consented to being put to death here on this planet to enable us pathetic microbes to develop into becoming the same as he is. I keep coming back to that. It really is impossible. That humans can be of such consequence to God he has been able to put up with us when every atom of his being must be repulsed by what we have become – is absurd. This race has become insane. God must know something we don't know. It is impossible Jesus did what he did just so we can go to Heaven when we die.

Well, there **is** a powerful reason why God needs us to be matured to becoming the same as Jesus is. We have hinted and also said plainly that he has been on a project for all Eternity past and it is time to begin stage 2. That is where we show up. This is where we move into the place we were in before there was a Creation Project.

If we could only see the heart of God Almighty, of what he has always planned and intended for us. If only we could see the magnitude of what Jesus actually accomplished on the cross. If only we could understand what Holy Spirit wants so desperately to pull together – we would change our minds about a lot of things very quickly.

CHAPTER EIGHT

GETTING TOGETHER
IS THE KEY

We have said that at its simplest, church is two people and God talking with each other. To be functional, the group will of necessity be larger but the church remains being that these people and God are sitting around, sipping coffee, and talking and interacting with each other. And that's it – just don't forget the coffee.

The point of these people and God sitting around talking with each other is that they have placed themselves into an environment where God is able to take them seriously and begin to restore them to being what he had infused of himself into Adam. We are designed and built to be, we are intended to be, exactly the same species of being as God himself is. Duplicates of God. If this is not happening, we need to be to where it is happening. This is why we get together like this. This is what our gathering exists to produce. That is why these people and God are sitting around talking with each other. There is a program being worked out that requires us to be so developed and equipped – and connected.

God has geared things on Earth so that he can do nothing without human involvement and the flip side of that arrangement is that we can do absolutely nothing without God. The original legal arrangement made between God and Adam giving humanity control of the affairs of Earth has never been cancelled and the intentions that humanity gain experience while they are doing that was never revoked. So, from his side, God is ready to get this job done. He is just waiting for us humans to get off our big fat pew and report for service.

This is so important. Can you imagine that Creator God built us to be the magnificent creatures we are, duplicates of all he is, to just mess around on Planet Earth as we are messing around on Planet Earth – let alone messing around in Heaven for Eternity. I am pretty sure that after the first few million years lolling around in our palatial celestial mansions, it could start to get tedious. God doesn't just sit around. Get yourself outside some nice dark night to see some of what he does in his spare time – or have a look at what is under your feet in the bright daylight.

Try to get locked into your gizzards that the amazing, humungous, majestically magnificent standard of creature we are is not made for lolling around for hundreds of thousands of millions of billions of trillions of eons in the luxurious mansions that have been prepared for us in Heaven. Eternity is for eternity. Eternity does not ever end. Think that through for a while. You will find you reach a place where your thinking can't take you any further. We humans aren't locked into Eternity mode yet.

Being copied to being the image and likeness of God is not so we can do what we are doing. Our involvement in the work-a-day business world is intended to be our apprenticeship, our boot camp, our place and time of preparation and training and gaining experience for the real work we are designed and intended to accomplish in the Grand Eternal Scheme of Things. That's why we are here on this planet at this time. This is part of our training and is giving us practice to be able to handle major responsibilities – and I had better leave it at that.

It's important to really get hold of the fact that when Jesus shouted from the cross – "**it is completely completed**" – every obstruction that had separated us from God was oblite-rated. The job had really been completely completed. Even 'perfectly perfected'. Let this awareness settle into your consciousness, because this is the only thing that sets you free and activates your get-up-and-go. Spend quality time with God right now and let the power of what was achieved on the cross take hold of you. It will change your life. It will change the world.

When Holy Spirit came to the 120 men and women that Pentecost Sunday morning – in Acts chapter 2 – and eventu-ally to us, the power and ability and wisdom to get things done was released into them – and us. We have no excuses. When we are not living in union of life with God Almighty, that is the choice we have made and it is not the responsibil-ity of any other person or event or situation or environment that you have made that choice.

Our group of men and women and youth and children getting together in a locality, who have allowed Holy Spirit to develop them into becoming duplicates of Jesus, is where we start. If we try to start something before we get there we will screw up. We cannot do anything – at all – until we have been developed into being those duplicates of Jesus. That is the starting point. More later.

As one who blew a lot of years and blood sweat and tears in useless denominational religiousness, let me tell you that you are wallowing in futility until you have deliberately set yourself to really and truly know God. I did not say anything about learning theology or Bible verses. I did that, and it doesn't work. God is not theology. Bible verses are not God. The Bible is not God. God is God and you start by setting yourself to know **him**. To attempt anything at all without having at least set yourself to reach the fullness of his intentions for you is to waste God's time and yours and to set yourself up for a crashing failure. **You can do nothing – at all – until you are filled through all your being with all the fullness of God.**

It is people trying to do things with religious stuff and Bible verses without first having deliberately set themselves to be developed into being made duplicates of Jesus and having that Holy Spirit power added to and working in and through them that has produced the mess we have in what was intended to be God's Church – and as a consequence – in our nations.

These people who are sitting around talking with God and each other are putting themselves into the position where Holy Spirit is able to re-direct their every word, thought and deed, hope, desire, ambition, goal, target, project, agenda, purpose, attitude, inclination or dream – everything – into alignment with the heart and mind of Christ and each other.

That should be easy.

It is the most difficult thing on Earth.

Folk coming into church – or even people who have been in church for decades – particularly those who believe they have "a ministry" – have their own program and agenda lurking in the back of their skull and are looking for opportunity to turn this loose. It happens all the time.

Right now on Planet Earth you will find it difficult to find two people able to agree with each other about anything. Any three church people have at least five opinions about everything. I mean – just listen to the carry-on inside your gizzards right now as you read this.

This is the massive problem that must be dealt with and resolved before anything can even begin to happen. There is no way around it and without that submission to Holy Spirit stripping you of all your grandiose ambitions, schemes, projects – everything – you are wasting your time and God's. We **must** come into alignment with each other and with God. If that doesn't happen, nothing is going to happen.

It is as we assemble together with God and allow Holy Spirit to reprogram us from the inside that our personal agendas are, kicking and screaming, dissolved. While we have a shred of our own ambition and program and goal remaining in us, we may as well forget the whole thing.

The job in hand at this point is to have that group of people in an area who have submitted themselves to Holy Spirit and each other to be moulded by him into being the Body of Christ in that area. Each person a component, a piece, a portion, which when assembled, becomes a functional operational structure. Never mind the big stuff. Get this sorted out before you attempt anything.

Let me say that a small group of people in unity with Holy Spirit and Jesus and Father and themselves could take this world apart in three weeks flat. A group of ten or twenty Holy Spirit filled duplicates of Jesus who have developed genuine heart unity with God and each other will discover there is nothing they cannot do. They can dismiss a government and install a government. They can stop an army. They can speak the world's stockpile of nuclear bombs into being buckets of beach sand. They can kill a cyclone/hurricane or bushfire. They can run a multilane highway across the middle of a sea or flatten a mountain into an airport or stop the planet rotating if that is what is needed right now. They are in fact, operating in and with the exact same force that brought Creation into being – which is the level of life God breathed into Adam with the intention it be passed on to us.

So – that initially, is what our assembled group is and what it is all about. A few people or a few thousand people or a few ten thousand people gathering to jump around and do religious things is not church and **it is most certainly not** the Body of Christ. The Body is composed of structural component members who **must** have seriously done business with God to the point they have become a union of life with him and have formed into being a vital functional piece of the assembled entity there that enables things to get done. And God will recognise those who have set their heart in that direction but still may have a way to go.

The genuine, functional Body of Christ in a local area is the representation of God Almighty in that area. They are there with him and for him and they demonstrate his Presence in that area – and that area knows it. And, of course, the aggregate of these local Bodies make up the locality-wide, suburb-wide, city-wide, nation-wide, and world-wide Body of Christ.

The Kingdom that God is preparing to break loose is a real visible and functional structured government that is being set up to regulate the affairs of nations and people on Planet Earth. The Kingdom is going to replace the insane satanic operations that are presuming to be "government" at this time. When the disciples asked Jesus to teach them to pray, the driving concern at the top of his heart intention came out as – "Pray for Father to remove existing wicked civil government and replace it with his righteous supervision. To abolish the existing evil thieving government control operations on Earth and replace it with the same order that regulates the affairs of Heaven". That's what he said. We call it "The Lord's Prayer" – and so it is.

CHAPTER NINE

THE MISSING COMPONENT

We have a problem. There is a vital component missing from everything needed to make what we have been talking about start to happen. The Missing Component is Holy Spirit himself.

To light a fire there must be a means of ignition. A match – a lighter – rubbing sticks together – there must be someone with something able to produce a spark that will ignite the fire.

In the early church those mentors we talked about had brought the Fire with them. Those men are not here anymore – nor have they been replaced – but without that fire having been lit, there will be no fire and any attempt to reproduce anything like was happening in the early church will end up being the schmozzle we currently have. You can't boil potatoes in cold water. There can be no presumptuous claiming a title or 'acting in faith' or 'seeing what God will do'. Jesus said that without him we can do nothing. Church has demonstrated the truth of those words for many centuries. It starts with Jesus. It starts with Holy Spirit. It starts when you realise you can do nothing by effort and programs or wanting. It must be God doing it. It must be God and you doing it together.

At this time in the Western world, I am not aware of ANYONE ANYWHERE who really does carry Holy Spirit fire and has the genuine capacity to transfer him to other people as was possible back in those early days. I acknowledge there are a lot of people around the Western world I don't know, but I am pretty sure I would have heard about it if they were around someplace.

In the current absence of having mentors like those early people were given, the first job, now at this time, is for our small group to deliberately set themselves to develop into becoming fire lighters – to make that connection – to have received Holy Spirit infusion for themselves – that "coming upon" that Jesus said would happen – and it must be real with evidence. The evidence is the ability to produce results: the evidence IS NOT "speaking in tongues".

Know and understand what you are setting out to do. Know and understand that you are putting yourself in God's hands, and that no amount of effort is going to produce anything but frustration. You are providing the environment, you are setting out to have Holy Spirit "come upon" you, and in that "coming upon" you will be given the connection and power and wisdom. You are setting out to have that flame ignited in you so you can pass it on to other prepared hearts.

You could start with just one friend – but unless that one friend is your sweetheart or spouse – men and women don't meet alone. Initially, try to be with a group of at least five with a maximum of ten who are all deliberately placing yourselves at the disposal of Holy Spirit.

That has happened a number of times that I am aware of since the early 1900s, but I am not aware of anything of Holy Spirit life and power that has remained from that. The problem being that folk at that time settled on the fact that "revival" was happening – and that was that – and every one of these happenings that I am aware of, died. These may whet our appetite, but we are aiming at what God has intended from the beginning and at what he intends with us here and now – and this time it is for keeps and it will not die. Avoid the word "revival". You are aiming at entering into fullness of life – that is – God's life filling and flooding every atom of your being. You are aiming at seeing Father's permanent national and international Kingdom come into existence – not a revival that is going to fade away very quickly. When Evan Roberts was persuaded to withdraw from the activities, the Welsh Revival died in one week.

What is required now is for that group to set themselves to provide the welcoming environment for Holy Spirit to "come upon" the men and women who are this group. If you were ever real and genuine and true in your life about anything – now is the time to go for him and not stop until Holy Spirit has met with you and has "come upon" you. At this time I believe Holy Spirit is running around the world looking for people who are genuinely looking for him. He is looking for small groups of people with hungry hearts and determination and stickability.

The basic mechanics of what I am aware of having happened during the past more than one hundred years that has resulted in Holy Spirit moving in and 'coming upon' the people waiting for him, have been similar.

In Wales, UK, Evan Roberts was a young coal miner with a small group of teenage friends who stuck with it until September 1904 when Holy Spirit moved in and the entire Principality of Wales became covered with a tangible Presence of Holy Spirit, the influence of which spread across much of the world.

In a round-about way that actually touched me thirty years later through association with converts of that revival who had migrated to Australia and moved to our town to work in the coal mines there and they became part of the church of which our family was part. Thirty years later, those fires were still burning. These were our family friends, and even as a child I loved to be where these people were. There was something about them that was good. In the church meetings when all these people were together, God came with them bringing a "Presence". When these Welsh and Scottish men and woman sang the old hymns in four or more part harmony – with no instruments – you had to be there. I found myself teary just remembering 70 and 80 years later. When our family moved from that district, I didn't encounter that Presence again for more than twenty years.

And some of that fire got into me and has caused me trouble all my life. Church can't stand young upstarts with fire in their bones. These days I'm an old upstart with fire in my bones, but Church still can't stand having upstarts around, regardless of vintage. You don't even have to say anything. You can't be real with God and be part of a church. It's really weird.

Back to here and now, it is Holy Spirit who is creating an awareness in a lot of people that it is time to get serious. It is the people in the group getting serious. It is finding yourself tangibly in the Presence of Holy Spirit. In many cases, the spark that sets things on fire has been as simple as the recognised beginning of the Welsh Revival, when just a few weeks after things had begun to happen, and people were starting to get together of an evening at the Old Moriah Chapel in Loughor in Wales, a young girl, Florrie Evans, who had been converted just that week, stood in the meeting and called – "I love the Lord Jesus with all my heart.". And as she said that – Holy Spirit "came upon" all those people gathered there – and that is recognised as being the spark that set much of the world on fire. Or in Argentina in the 1950s, in a small meeting of less than ten people, it was a lady thumping a table that triggered what is still a move of God that has been spreading up through South America for more than sixty years and is still growing. There was a lot more to the story than thumping the table, but it was that simple act of obedience that set a massive "move" in motion. NO – don't thump a table or tell Jesus you love him to try to start something. It won't work.

In the histories of "moves" God has made since the turn of the twentieth century, in Topeka Kansas for instance, a group of men and women set themselves to discover what was that missing element in their lives and ministry. The last week of 1899 they had spent the whole time searching for what the Bible said about this matter. They became really serious with God and made the discovery that the answer to their search is to be 'come upon by Holy Spirit' like the folk in the upper room had experienced. So they set themselves to receive that infusion but did not know what to do. In the very first hour of 1900 – within an hour of that century turning – a girl named Agnes Ozman asked Charles Parham, the group leader, to "lay hands" on her, which he reluctantly did, but when he did, Agnes received such an immersion in Holy Spirit she literally lit up and was speaking in tongues and was unable to speak in English for three days. That was the beginning of what became the Pentecostal/Charismatic movement that virtually covers the Earth today. That led to an 'African American' preacher, William Seymour, coming into contact with Charles Parham in Texas six years later, and who then moved to California. What is known as the Azusa Street Revival that covered Los Angeles beginning 1906 resulted from that meeting between Charles Parham and William Seymour. Charles Parham was the firelighter for that revival, although he had no personal involvement in it.

And all that began as the result of a group of people getting serious with God back in Topeka six years earlier. That is what I am talking about. Although what became the Pentecostal/Charismatic movement grew in numbers, and is still growing in numbers, the fire they carried in those early days did not last very long. By the 1920s, it was just another religion group – and still is – and totally useless. OK – look around you before you start chucking bricks.

What I am saying is, that the critical need right now is for Holy Spirit to be able to find that group of men and women and teens and children who will provide the environment that will welcome him to move into the situation and meet with them and get that blaze started. You must be real. No pretence. And stick with it until he comes.

There have been other moves of Holy Spirit during the past more than one hundred years, and when you read the stories, always in the background there is that group of men and women who have stuck with it until He came. And usually, there was that one insignificant act that triggered the response.

I am pretty sure that some of you reading this will decide to pray for a Pentecost happening in your area. Just make yourself available, and God will tell you what to do.

The "coming upon" Jesus promised *IS NOT* the Pentecostal "baptism in Holy Spirit". There was life there on several occasions a hundred years ago, but the fire has long since died and in the Western world, it no longer exists. All that remains now is mostly religion professionals telling people what they want to hear – particularly, how to get rich.

Let me plead with you. There MUST be men and women who have possibly even been "hidden in caves" for a long time waiting and crying for Holy Spirit to make his move. Ask him to connect you with at least one other similar cave dweller. But be real. No pretence. No imagining you are the modern John Lake or Charles Finney. They have been and done it and gone.

Several years ago I was in England and had some spare days so I rented a car and went out to Wales. I had no problem finding Loughor and the Old Moriah Chapel where that Revival fire had burst into flame. It is said that from that night when it all began, the doors of that chapel did not close for three years, there was a constant gathering of people in the chapel for three years. I wanted to know if there was any lingering Presence from the days when this building was the centre from which Holy Spirit covered the entire Principality, the influence of which moved far beyond.

It was dead.

The building is very old. It's name was the OLD Moriah Chapel in 1904, and it is really ugly. The front yard is full of the graves of dead people. There is a bust of Evan Roberts near the entrance gate. The main vehicle gate was a big rusty affair with a big rusty chain holding it shut and was locked with an even bigger rusty padlock.

I was out on the footpath crying when God started talking and telling me that what had happened there was for that place at that time. What he has prepared for me will be in my place and in my time. At 85 as I write this, I am getting curious.

What I am saying is that whatever God does with you will be what God does with YOU. It will not be a copy of anything that has happened at any other time. Although I have given very brief histories of the way he has moved in recent centuries, my only point is that the 'coming upon' in each case I am aware of, was the result of a small group of people creating the welcoming environment and making themselves available for Holy Spirit to make his move.

This is the most important thing in the world right now – it is the most important thing in the history of the world. It's Kingdom time. It's Body of Christ time. Where are the men – particularly the men – and women and young people? Holy Spirit is roaming the planet looking for people to call his release into his church and into his nations and into his world. I know what I have said is hopelessly inadequate, but go after Holy Spirit with everything you've got – relentlessly – and don't ever give up.

If what is churning around inside me is any indication, I think we can expect to see some interesting events starting to happen around the world – possibly even by the time this book hits the pavement.

Whatever God is putting together at this time is wholly dependent on Holy Spirit bringing the pieces together. We can't organize it. We can't work it up. We can't make it happen. But as the folk within that group mature and let go their personal ambitions and agendas, Holy Spirit will be releasing himself into them – and the abilities we talked about a couple of chapters back will begin to develop.

The ultimate key to everything is you getting to know God himself as a Person. The **real** business is done when you are home alone, just you and God. He knows your heart and he will respond to your heart that is truly aching to really know him. Then, when you get together with your teammates the sparks will fly.

As you develop this relationship with each other you will discover Holy Spirit is sharing secrets with you. You will know things you have no way of knowing. You are beginning to realise that what Paul called "the fruit of the Spirit" is developing in you. The love and joy and peace, the patience, gentleness, goodness, the meekness, faithfulness and Godly self-control, are changing the way you see things and do things. You will get to understand that what Christ living inside you is working on is to produce in you the personality and character of the very Spirit of Holiness himself, and that he is drawing you into becoming "as he is". He is making you to be a union of life with himself. You are going to find your-self spending a lot of time worshipping Lord God Most High in Spirit and in Truth on your face on the floor of your bed-room – or more probably on your bed, – at home and in utter silence. Noise will be as repulsive to you as it is to God.

Get to really KNOW God. He is your source of everything, and day-by-day, we see more of the wonder and perfection of God and his intentions, of Jesus and his character, of Holy Spirit and his beauty of holiness. The old stuff we used to live with gets to be very unattractive. We move on until we realise there is a dimension in our life that goes way past anything we even knew existed. We are starting to get there. The character is beginning to develop that will enable God to achieve some very interesting results as we work together with him.

By this time, the group of you getting together after having lived in that connection with Holy Spirit at home, will release a force that will produce some amazing results. What I am talking about now is what will begin to happen as The Kingdom takes over and the Body of Christ has come alive and Holy Spirit begins to cover the localities where you live. As the move gains momentum, you can expect to be having visits from Jesus. You will be getting to know the angels who have been assigned to work with you. A "Presence" of Holy Spirit will radiate out from you and draw people to you – as was happening in Wales during the 1904-5 Revival.

During the Welsh Revival, Holy Spirit "Presence" settled over that entire Principality. People coming into Wales from England by train knew they had crossed the border. They could feel the "Presence". The same "Presence" was said to have covered Los Angeles during the time of the Azusa Street revival a couple of years later.

It will be like that.

You will be meeting with God. He has been waiting for you. You will experience involvement with God Himself. He will finish anything still not completed. And let God trust you to finish what you have started. We have entered the Kingdom of God era. A whole new life has begun and we can never go back. Things are going to start showing. Prayers are being answered. God is talking to you and discussing the current situation he has involved you with. He may tell you to sack a politician – or a government – or close a chain of stores. Or to stop a storm or a cyclone or a flood or bushfire. There is nothing you can't do. When the teams minister – what you are doing will happen.

It will be like that.

I will just comment at this point, that although what I am saying here possibly sounds pretty much airy-fairy-wishful-thinking and unrelated to reality – everything I have said has happened as isolated incidents in different locations around the world at different times in the past century – some of it involving situations and people I have known.

I will also comment that you are not going to get much encouragement from the religion industry. They are not on your side and will go to great lengths to ridicule and condemn you – and stop you. Once you begin to get serious with God, you will not be able to remain involved with church. God and church are not in the same business.

CHAPTER TEN

GETTING IT WORKING

Jesus said we would receive power when Holy Spirit came upon us. He said we would be doing greater things than he did. He said we could move mountains. It has never happened in the Western church.

Jesus told us he would answer our prayers that our joy may be full – that the Father may be glorified in the Son. I don't know – and have never known – **anyone** who consistently gets their prayers answered. For sure, I am personally aware of continual protection – sometimes miraculous protection – for my family and myself and of occasional instruction in my life and affairs and I have seen amazing things happen on **extremely** rare occasions.

That is not the way Jesus lived and that is NOT what Jesus said. He said we would have what we asked for. This has been bugging me since I was a kid when I heard the preachers whom I knew, making all those promises that didn't happen for me or them or anyone else. I know there is the issue of believing that you receive what you ask for – but even that depends on God releasing his faith in us. We don't get prayers answered by screwing up our eyes real tight and clenching our fist and wishing real hard. The whole process is of God. The trick goes right back to connecting with him. Everything is tied into that connection.

It seems to me that Father God has been holding all this in reserve waiting for us to deliberately set ourselves to be transformed into becoming of the measure of the stature of the fullness of Christ – duplicates of Jesus. I know that God is not going to release himself into a bunch of half-baked religion devotees who are still locked into the system and their programs. He needs us to develop into that level of maturity and identification with him so he can trust us with big stuff.

This is what I have come to understand. There are all those "promises" in the New Testament. We have been taught all our lives that we can "claim" those promises for ourselves, because this is the "word of God" and the word of God doesn't lie – so we must get what we have asked for. I mean, God is obligated to do as we say.

It doesn't work like that. Those promises were not given to you. When Jesus made those statements to his team that is who the promises were intended for. Jesus was speaking "rhema" to them. That is the word God is speaking to these people in this situation at this time. You weren't there. All you have now is "logos" which is something spoken to some-one else about something else at some other time. "Logos" does not produce results. That is why Jesus told his crew at the fig tree incident in Mark 11, that they needed to have "the faith OF God". Not "faith IN God" as KJ tells you.

Having faith "IN God" does not achieve much. We come right back to what I have been saying – we can do nothing unless it is a cooperative act between God and you. It is your connection and relationship with God that makes things happen – NOT how many Bible promises you have memorised or can quote back to God.

Right now, for virtually anyone in the Western world to be getting prayers answered would create disastrous chaos. While we are living in "**me**" mode, God is keeping his lid on what we get up to. We are supposed to be **developing** into being as God is. And God is not releasing his goodies until we are.

Trust Holy Spirit. He is behind all this and he will finish what he started. You can't hurry him. You can't push him. He wants this done properly so he takes the time to get the details right. Of course, this can – and does – produce frustration and impatience in us that gets pretty hard to live with and sometimes makes us hard to live with. But I know that the time is with us when we can expect things to start happening that have never happened before. When you as a group reach that point of harmony and resonance as you and Holy Spirit fellowship with each other – it will happen. It is getting ready to happen as you are getting ready for it to happen.

When Holy Spirit arrived early that Pentecost Sunday morning in AD 33, he had burned himself into each of the 120 men and women who and been upstairs for ten days waiting for him as Jesus had told them to. Those days of waiting and expecting had produced a welcoming environment for him, so that as the prophetic clock ticked over to the Day of Pentecost, Holy Spirit arrived on cue. As he and those waiting men and women are fused together, the sparks are visibly flying, and the effect of that encounter spread city-wide within the hour.

It will be like that.

By nine o'clock the whole city and its visitors are filling the street out the front, and they are frightened. There have been supernatural events happening in Jerusalem for two months and the whole population – and their visitors – are seriously spooked.

Around daylight this morning they have heard the terrifying sound like from a jet aircraft taking off. It is only eight weeks since they are lining the road leading into Jerusalem, spreading their coats and palm fronds on the roadway where Jesus was riding his borrowed donkey into town and they are shouting "Hosanna to the Son of David. Blessed is he who comes in the name of the Lord. Hosanna in the highest." It's only seven weeks since these same people are standing in the crowd yelling "Crucify Him". They have watched the sickening spectacle of Jesus being executed. They are terrified as that thick darkness came over the whole area at noon and remained until three o'clock the afternoon of the crucifixion while Jesus was still on the cross. They have all poured out to the cemetery that Resurrection Sunday morning and have seen the cocoon of linen cloth Jesus had been wrapped in, lying in the crypt still holding the shape of his body. People they know have actually seen Jesus after he had come back to life. They are edgy and they are scared.

Now this! All these men and women are out in the street "giving clear and loud expression" as the power of Holy Spirit is surging through them – enabling them to "tell all the mighty works of God" in languages that were understood by each of the people from the different countries visiting there – who knew quite well these Galilean natives speaking did not know their language or "particular dialect". (" " Amp. NT)

When Peter spoke to the crowd, a Holy Spirit infused, gut-wrenching guilt and conviction and shame and horror and terror came over them as they realised they had actually shouted for God to be crucified – followed by very real Holy Spirit imparted repentance. Three thousand of them acknowledged that Jesus really is God – and received him as their Messiah and Saviour right there right then – and were baptised in public to let the world know they meant business. The Church of Jesus Christ was born and came into existence in that hour that Pentecost Sunday morning.

It will be like that.

When Holy Spirit keeps his appointment with you who are being prepared and waiting, the whole city is going to know about it very quickly. Things are going to start happening where you live. You have now become the functional BODY OF CHRIST – that is, the Body of people in whom Jesus is living in that location. And being the Body of Christ in that location you are the operational resident Representation of God Almighty in your area. Holy Spirit is now free to release himself into you and among you – **and out from among you into your neighbourhood and city and nation.**

The Kingdom of God has come. The Emperor has returned and retaken his Empire. He re-establishes national laws on Earth to be those that regulate the way things are done at The Palace.

It's getting ready to happen.

A local result will be that the assembly of God's people in that street – because they are a unified body or group – have become the local government in that area. They are The Authority in that area. They look after each other. The body takes responsibility for the people and situations in their area. In essence, that little group of households is its own police force, court-house, welfare centre, local council, working together with God Almighty and each other to minister righteousness and responsibility in that neighbour-hood.

In your area, there will be no justification for dead people to stay dead, for sick people to stay sick, for kids to be in rebel-lion, for Godless governments and their evil bureaucracies to be killing, stealing and destroying everything they touch. Things will never be the same.

It hasn't happened there yet? Stick with it. I said several pages back that a missing element in almost all our lives has been that we have never received the completeness of what Jesus intended when he said we would "receive power when Holy Spirit is come upon you".

Hang in there. It's getting ready to happen on a scale that will not only astound you but will astound and frighten everyone who even hears about what you have done.

Jesus intended we would operate on a level not less than that which he did. He actually arranged that we would do greater things than he did. We were originally built to be a supernatural people and are intended to be a supernatural people, able with Holy Spirit to "do super-abundantly, far over and above all that we dare ask or think, infinitely beyond our highest prayers, desires, thought, hopes or dreams" – as we have quoted several times already.

God is so huge. I try to understand him sometimes, but my understanding doesn't even make it to the end of the block. His Eternity and Creation are so incomprehensively massively huge, his plans for us human people are so incredibly huge they are way past our ability to even imagine. God built Betelgeuse and he made electrons – and zygotes. How can we ever know him. Those galaxies recently discovered by the Hubble infrared Ultra Deep Field exploration are up to ten billion light-years distant from Earth. Try to get your head around the Jesus you know being out there ten billion years ago building those things. Gentle Jesus meek and mild and all that. What I am saying here and elsewhere is trying to get us to catch a glimpse of the magnitude of what we are involved in. Our pathetic little religion games just make God spew. Yes – that's in the Bible too.

This time you will operate in that same authority as is resident in God Almighty – in whose image and likeness we were built. Having developed into becoming of the measure of the stature of the fullness of Christ, you are now in the position where the creative power breathed into you by the Creator of All Creation can be released. To get things started, you have now begun the work of getting this planet back in the hands of To Whom it Belongs.

As we move with God, being the supernatural people we have become, and as we operate in Kingdom of God's authority and with Kingdom of God's dynamos power, the prayer Jesus gave his disciples as a pattern will begin to be fulfilled. Things are being made ready to change on this planet.

What I am REALLY talking about is what God is setting up to be normal in his people – and ultimately in all people around the world. This is it. It's on. This is not a new church. This is Creator God turning his newly activated and empowered Body loose on Planet Earth – and he has made you to be part of himself and with him, to be part of this tremendous adventure.

I see the existing industrial commercial religion industry as being something like Ezekiel's valley of dry bones. Actually, the existing Western church would be several degrees deader than Ezekiel's dry bones (in Ezekiel 37). It's beyond redemption. I mean – what do you do with acres of dry bones except grind them up and plough them into the paddock as calcium fertiliser. But – when God moves into the situation, anything can happen and the bones become an army. I believe the new-born Body of Christ will come together as did that army of dry bones.

Ezekiel was told to prophesy, and as he did there was a stirring and a rattling and bones came flying from all over to connect with his neighbour bone, and sinews and flesh and skin covered the skeletons until there was a whole army standing there – alive and ready to do business.

Some of you prophets – set yourself in position and remain on standby waiting for *that command* to prophesy to that mess of dead bones. It's going to happen.

CHAPTER ELEVEN

LET'S GET REAL
SERIOUS NOW

We are of consequence to God beyond human capacity to imagine. He fixed things so we could develop a real relationship with Him and for us to just fritter our life away; to wholly ignore God and Eternity, and the fact that our less than one hundred years here is the only time we are given to develop intimacy with God and prepare for Eternity – that is so frightening. Eternity – never ending, eternal Eternity is going to be a long time. Ten billion years from now you will probably still be regretting that you ignored God and trifled away your hundred years boot camp.

We know that God has been on a major development project for billions of years and you can see a bit of where he has been. He has been taking the weekend off for a few thousand years, maybe even a few million years, what difference would it make, but he is making preparation for the next stage and it is very obvious to me that Planet Earth is the site office from which this stage will be launched.

That's why God made us. We humans are custom built for this specific purpose. We are the only species of beings who are made in the "image and likeness" of God himself and we had to be made this way so we would have the capacities needed so we can do what we are being prepared to do.

We are built to be super beings – doing things like "superabundantly, far over and above all that we dare ask or think, infinitely beyond our highest prayers, desires, thoughts, hopes or dreams." We are told that we can do greater things than Jesus did. We are told we can tell a mountain to go jump into the ocean and it will obey us. We are supposed to be achieving things at that level. And that's just for getting us into practice while we are still here.

There's not much happening at that level at this time, but I believe it will become normal very quickly. Father's Kingdom is being set up to take over on Earth. In the ultimate big picture, it is vital we be able to do what God can do, which is why we are made to the same as he himself is. Jesus was not fantasising when he made those statements, and I am not fantasising when I quote him.

I will say again that Father God had us in his heart long before he began the Creation project. There is a good foundation for us to know that we humans have been specifically designed and built on this planet to become part of the development project I am calling Creation Stage 2. The information hidden here and there is sufficient to let us know that we are deliberately purpose-built and are being groomed to be national, international and intergalactic administrators, regulators and developers – and yea verily – creators. We need to be able to arrive on a property to which we have been assigned, and say "Atmosphere Be! Water Be! Vegetation Be!" – just like our GM can.

I know I hinted at this earlier, but by now you have either broken out in goose-bumps and maybe jumped around a bit – or you now have conclusive evidence that this clown has lost his marbles.

I spent enough years in the religion world to have a pretty good idea what many of you are saying right now. But, as I will challenge a bit further on – if you think I am wrong – you tell us what was the point of humans ever having been put on this planet. And do at least twenty years thinking and listening before you tell us.

Anyway, let's assume you made the grade and have settled into your palatial mansion in the Heavens, and you are really enjoying the company and environment. And one hundred years go by – then one thousand years go by – then a million years go by – then one hundred million years go by – and you are starting to get bored.

God Almighty did not make you a duplicate of himself just so you could sit on a fluffy white cloud and strum a geetah for Eternity. Jesus did not submit himself to the horrors of the cross on your behalf so you can just snuggle into the paradisal sheets on your celestial foam mattress nor generally loll around forever in that fancy spread of yours.

Do yourself a favour and do a bit of thinking and listening. No – don't ask the experts – they are in a worse mess than you are. Don't waste months pulling your King James to bits trying to prove what I am saying is wrong. Do your own thinking and listening – and keep thinking and listening until you get answers. I say again, that Jesus gave us Holy Spirit to be our source of information – not any written material – at all!!! **Jesus did not give us the New Testament. A Roman emperor named Constantine gave us the New Testament in 331 AD., Jesus gave us Holy Spirit.** He is your source of information – ultimately, your ONLY source of information.

Let me get really – literally – off the planet with you for a couple of minutes. I am sure enough to dare stick my neck out. Fifty five years ago, at age thirty, **I deliberately set out to discover what God was up to when he made Adam.** This adventure has been built on the previous thirty years of exposure to and eventual participation in, solid evangelical doctrinal teaching since infancy. Then for the past fifty five years I have dug and searched and listened and dug some more.

The result being that I have come to a point of being very sure that Creator God made us with the specific intention that we, working together with him, are intended to colonise and to populate and develop as a long term project – a real long term project – every one of the potentially habitable satellites out there, and the endless enormousness of never-ending Eternity ahead is quite enough time to get that all done. There – I said it.

The existence of the human race makes no sense whatever otherwise.

Jesus did not submit himself to crucifixion just so we can sit around in Heaven for million and billions and trillions of eons. God doesn't sit around. He is the ultimate working class – and he made us the same as he is. Think it through before you start throwing things.

Before I was thirty I knew as much Bible and evangelical teaching as you know and from time to time was even speaking in denominational conferences – and our church experience was just as pointless and useless as yours is now. That is why I set out to discover what God was really up to when he made we humans on Planet Earth. If God does something there is a reason behind it. He doesn't very often tell us what that reason is and leaves us to find out for ourselves what that may be.

So – keep asking yourself why God made you like he is – in his image and after his likeness? I mean – what would be the point? A copy of God is a *very* consequential class of being. Being made with the intention we be part of the family and household of God is beyond anything possible on Earth. But that's what he did. That's what we are. But why????

Then after we had really messed up, why didn't he just write us off as another bad batch? Except for eight people, he wiped out the entire population of the planet on one occasion – and there was a very good reason for doing that, which is a very different subject. He wiped out the entire population of two cities another time It is possible that Jesus submitted himself to the barbarity of his crucifixion – so that among other things – we pathetic losers need not be wiped out again – and – as hopelessly incredible as that possibility may be – so we could in fact be restored right back to the original intention? You think you have God all worked out – don't kid yourself. There are a lot of things going on that we don't know about. You don't know either. Keep reading.

Church was developed to enable us to be restored to being of the measure of the stature of the fullness of Christ. That is – being returned to God's original intention when he made people. We are a very significant class of created beings and we didn't ought to be in the mess we are in.

The big immediate issue we are facing right now at this time is Father's Kingdom being set up. I said earlier that Jesus is recorded to have mentioned church only one time, but he is recorded as having spoken about his Father's Kingdom around one hundred times. If you gather these statements together, and with what he was saying about kings and rulers and reigning and much more along those lines, a pattern emerges. Kings. Thrones. Ruling. Reigning. That's not the language of the unwashed masses. There's upper crust involved in those words. Sons and daughters of Lord God Most High. Come on people. Princes and Princesses? How much more upper crust can you be? We are made for involvement with Father God and his eternal intentions – and that intention is NOT for you to be growing barnacles on your backside either down here or up there.

Working with Father as he sets up his Kingdom in the here and now is going to be an exciting adventure. Father God is taking over and we are here to be part of him as he is doing it and picking up some valuable experience while we are at it.

Affairs on Earth are eventually going to wind down and we

will be out in Creation Stage 2 where we are built to ultimately be. It is going to be fun watching all that real estate come alive.- and without claiming a "thus saith the Lord" I am satisfied that this is the situation.

After having spent a lot of decades observing the awesome wonders of Creation here on this micro planet, I cannot believe God Almighty has spent an Eternity building all those squillion billion galaxies out there just to while away a bit of time. Just this one tiny planet is absolutely crammed with marvels that demonstrate his Father-heart – and sense of humour. I think we are going to see a lot more of both when we get out there.

Meanwhile, back on Planet Earth, there is a Bible verse that is really out of place in the book of Habakkuk (2:14) Stuck in the middle of a litany of woes and pending doom, and completely out of context, Habakkuk says. "But the time is coming when the earth shall be filled with the knowledge of the glory of the Lord as the waters cover the sea." The very next word being "Woe to him who gives his neighbour drink."

Not since Noah has the world seen a mess such as we have at this time in history. There is doom and gloom and every form of wickedness you can imagine – and a lot you could never imagine. There is extreme wickedness in high places all over the planet. It was while he was in the middle of his local version of this situation that Habakkuk was living with, he came up with that one ray – just a glimmer – of a better day coming.

I believe that about now in world history, we are going to see God put on a show that is going to undo a very great deal of mischief on this planet and I intend to see this in my lifetime and I am 85 as I write this.

This is God's world. He gave us the responsibility to govern it for him. We are a consequential bunch of people We are God's people – made in his image – regardless of what we have let ourselves degenerate into being. And when God makes his move, there are going to be some big changes – and the physical, observable glory of God – not just the knowledge of it – is going to spread across this planet as the waters cover the sea. In a vision I was given nearly 30 years ago I saw that happen in this godless nation of Australia, and I watched that glory spreading in all directions until the whole continent was covered with the Glory of God, and every person in this nation was caught up in it and standing there, hands in the air, worshipping their God Almighty. It's going to happen, and I'm going to see it. The spark that started that was not any particular location or group or action. It was that the Body of Christ had been restored to being the Body of Christ allowing Holy Spirit to move in – and turn this entire nation right-way-up. That's going to happen, but the resurrected Body of Christ will bear no resemblance to the old industrial commercial religious stuff. Not even the same buildings. Mainly in the living rooms or back verandas in the street block where you live.

So – at this time we have this planet being restored to the original intention – and we have the vastness of Creation out there ready to be set up so Creator God's intention as he was building all that is now being made ready to happen. As I said early in this material, it was we people in Father's heart who were the motivation for the incredible display of his majesty and glory he came up with. He was doing it for us. I believe that for all Eternity God has intended that all Creation – including Planet Earth – will be filled with his glory as the vastness of space and all Creation is filled with his presence and will be filled with his people – and that glory is radiating out from us. Out in the Creation Stage 2 project, we will not be contaminated with Earth crud. Out there, God in us is not being blocked from shining out from within us. It will just be normal for us all the time like it is normal for God all the time. I repeat, we are made the same as God is.

I am aware that Jesus said that in the Resurrection men and women don't marry but I am not talking about the Resurrection. I am talking about our Creator's eternal intentions. If what I have come to understand is the way it will be, then a new phase will develop as has happened so many times previously – as will be sort of necessary if he wants a population that is fruitful and multiplying and filling Creation. A hilarious thought emerges. If you were to have a baby every thousand years, in one million years, you could have had one thousand babies. Or if you had a baby every one hundred years, in a million years, that would be ten thousand babies – or every ten years – aw – come on – that would be one hundred thousand babies – then the next million – and billion. Birthday parties, grand kids – the mind boggles. But we are talking about Eternity and that is going to be very, very different to our Earth times. In part of my "prophetic stories" that will follow the publication of this book I describe what it could be like with people, both those from Earth as living humans setting up the first colony who are joined by a group of humans who have been residing in Heaven as spirits of dead people for hundreds of years, but who have been brought out to Sagi One and restored to being humans again, as the new project gets under way out in the Sagittarius constellation. It was fun watching a barren planet– and those restored humans – come to life.

I know there are "end time" prophecies in circulation, but as with most things derived from written material, there are as many versions of what is going to happen as there are people trying to make sense of the prophecies.

In any case, there have been many phases during Earth's human history and I have no trouble seeing changes happening as the new stage of Creation is ready to kick in.

Let me say plainly that, to me at least, it is pretty apparent that we humans are purpose built to ultimately colonise, develop and populate each of the suitable satellite planets scattered throughout Creation. And there are a lot of them.

NOW – I am perfectly aware that by now a lot of folk are chucking wobblies. But before you set up the inquisition, or call for the men in white coats – *please* – *be my guest* – *you tell it.*

Meanwhile, make yourself comfortable and do some thinking.

Where do you expect to be, and what do you expect to be doing the afternoon of April 15, AD 782,573,947?

Why do you think God has placed that massive complexity of Creation in the heavens? Billions of galaxies, some more than ten billion light-years distant from Earth? Just to look pretty??? Before the Hubble infrared camera, we didn't even know those newly discovered galaxies were there – so looking pretty is not it.

A consideration" If we wanted to explore some of those distant galaxies and we were able to travel at the speed of light – that is 670,616,629 miles per hour – to get there – it could take us ten billion years to arrive at our destination. I think I said somewhere that our God is very big. He does it in a micro-second. The folk in that prophetic story I told you about, who are setting up that first colony out in Sagittarius - which is 20,000 light years distance from Earth – flit back and forth from Sagi One to Earth in an instant. When you are built the same as God is, you can do that.

Let me remind you again that you are an eternal creature and that you will be alive somewhere doing something for ALL eternity.

I have said all this to get you thinking. So – do a spot of thinking and listening. Your answers will come from God – not from any other source of information – including this.

CHAPTER TWELVE

GOD HAS AN AGENDA
AND YOU ARE PART OF IT

Meanwhile, back to here and now on Planet Earth, there was that one thing Jesus talked about more than any other. It is Father's Kingdom and that is our item of interest right now.

A "Kingdom" is a Government. We are talking about a literal Government operating on Planet Earth and the Head of that Government is the KING – Father God Almighty Himself. You have heard about the proposed "one world government" – well – this might not be what those promoters had in mind, but this is it. Father's Kingdom is the real One World Government.

A lot of writings from highly regarded teachers speak of the Kingdom of God as though this is a functional fact on Earth right now. They seem to be missing that Jesus asked his men to pray for Father's Kingdom to *come*. Something *coming* would be an event. As far as I am aware, that event has never occurred. With that coming of the Kingdom, the way things are regulated in Heaven become the way things are done on Earth – and that would be accompanied by power and glory. I would hate to think that the way things are happening on Earth right now is the way things are done in Heaven. And I'm not seeing much power or glory on Earth right now either.

The coming of Father's Kingdom is the next part of the agenda to kick into place – it will be an event – and I believe that is imminent. You can read all about it in the third of the series of my stories.

The authority of civilian government regulating the affairs on Planet Earth given to Adam and his progeny will now be returned under God to where it is supposed to be.

Working together with Father God and Jesus and Holy Spirit and the Body of Christ, with Kingdom authority we are initially involved in undoing the entire devilish destructive, thieving control operation our "governments" have become, and then installing the Godly and God-appointed and God-ordained men to take over and be regulating the affairs of our nations as affairs are regulated in Heaven.

The Kingdom of God on Earth is of paramount significance to the ultimate eternal intentions of Father God. He literally established Planet Earth to be the site office and work base from which Creation Stage 2 will be launched and in the early days, be administered.

That is why we humans were set up on this planet. Tiny little Earth and its inhabitants are of tremendous consequence in the Grand Eternal Scheme Of Things. It is on this planet that Father God has arranged to establish his Kingdom so people could know and understand the way he operates. So people could get practice and gain skills in responsible government. Where people could exercise their built-in God-ingrained creativity and inventiveness and constructive abilities.

We know that Jesus set up the Church to be the force that would bring the whole planet back under the dominion of Father God. For two thousand years the church has not done this, but now at this time the force of God's assembled people is going to return the nations of Earth back into the hands of Jesus so Jesus can restore it back to Father – so that Father God can once again be God-Over-All – as Paul told us in 1st Corinthians 15. **Yes he did – just quit yer arguin' and pay attention. I'm lernin' ya sumpin.**

Did you know this verse is in the Bible? This is the hand-over ceremony, which cannot happen until the nations are first in the hands of Jesus. Revelation 11:15 – **"The seventh angel blew his trumpet, and there was a mighty voice in Heaven, shouting. 'The dominion, kingdom, sovereignty, rule of the world has now come into the possession and become the kingdom of our Lord and of His Christ, the Messiah, and he shall reign forever and ever, for the eternity of the eternities'."**

I am saying that it is the business of the Body Of Christ to lay the groundwork for this handing-over ceremony.

SO – all that has been said in all the previous chapters brings us to this point. We are at the time NOW when our business is to get the nations back into the hands of Jesus. This is why this new breed of sons and daughters of God Almighty are being equipped as no generation before has ever been equipped.

This is the job we have been assigned at this time. Nothing is capable of being achieved until we assembled sons and daughters of Father God have reached that point of being equipped to the level of maturity and identification with him that God intends – and requires. As I have been hammering throughout this book, this maturity is developed through the interaction of the Holy Spirit gifted and equipped and empowered men and women and teenagers and children working together in the Body of Christ with Holy Spirit and ending up with what is nothing less than Jesus Christ himself being duplicated and multiplied in each of the members of all the Body and so becoming the functional Representation of God Almighty on Planet Earth.

SO – we end up being the representation of God Almighty on this planet. We even look the part. We walk like God, we talk like God, we love like God, we get things done like God. Those watching us cannot tell where we leave off and where God starts. We are a union of life with God Almighty, with Father and Jesus and Holy Spirit filling and flooding every particle of our being.

We reach the point of knowing we are, and are living as being, righteous with his righteousness. Holy with his holiness. Perfect with his perfection. Holy minds. Holy boldness to the point of violence – and the power of the Resident Creator-of-Betelgeuse within us enabling it all to happen. That's the way it was always supposed to be. That is what Jesus set up.

There can be no limits and no restrictions.

What we – God's people – the genuine Body of Christ people – are facing now is infinitely more challenging than anything anyone of earlier generations have had to deal with. We are face to face with the unadulterated forces of satan the devil deeply imbedded into the entire operation of the affairs of Planet Earth – I mean – **everything**.

But built into each one of us is the intrinsic force that produced all Creation breathed into Adam when he was being made, which was lost when Adam deliberately disobeyed, but which was restored to us through the deliberate obedience of the Second Adam, Jesus, as he Completely Completed all that was required to get us back to where we were supposed to be. What Jesus had achieved on the cross, and confirmed when he returned from being dead, and which was re-activated on the Day of Pentecost – was the turning point of human history. It happened.

No more excuses.

The situation is nicely summed up for us in 2 Corinthians 4 – "**All of us are constantly being transfigured into Christ's very own image in ever increasing splendour and from one degree of glory to another, for this comes from the Lord who is the Spirit**".

This is what God Almighty is up to with us right now. We are being equipped to be involved in getting this planet back into the hands of God Almighty – **and** – for the Glory of God to begin covering the planet as the waters cover the seas – and ultimately throughout all Creation – **and** – each of us attaining to that measure of the stature of the fullness of Christ is where we start.

Intimacy with God himself, at home, alone with God, is the foundation for everything that happens when you get to the Body gathering. It is that one on one contact where the union and identification is developed. And that development is what brings us to Father's original intention. When a group of people who have grown into that level of union of life with God get together – something is going to bust loose.

There is a tangible force at work. When live and compatible electrical or electronic or chemical or mechanical components are connected, an action occurs, a resonance, a harmonizing happens. It is that resonance, that harmony, that blending together of precision tuned forces, that makes things work. A modern motor vehicle or aircraft is a good example of all these components co-operating in harmony.

When God Almighty is the one who assembles and tunes that arrangement of men and women who have allowed Holy Spirit to mature them into becoming duplicate-of-Jesus components, you are going to know that things will never be the same.

And **that** is the man and woman who is going to see the Kingdom come, and God's will being done on Planet Earth. And **that** is the man and woman who is being groomed to operate with responsible government authority in Creation Stage 2.

And **that** is what I am talking about.

SO, Father has this army of Warrior Princes and Princesses, intimate Sons and Daughters of Lord God Most High, set up and made combat ready, in union of being with all that is Holy and Glorious and Powerful.

Jesus said it is the violent who will be taking the Kingdom by force.

It is war, there will be opposition, and there will be violence.

Because what I've been talking about here **really** upsets the devil. There are some vicious entities out there, both human and spirit – and hybrids. They are powerful beings, and their fury against God Almighty is absolute and when they see you and they know you are in the place where they should be and doing what they were supposed to be doing – that makes them cranky.

At this point in our secular and church history-in-the-making the devil and his forces are advancing across the planet like a bushfire. This is a two-pronged assault. On one side is the banker family/one world government gang and on the other, Islam is on the march across the world – including your country and mine. Nothing of substance is opposing either of them.

It is a very one-sided, lop-sided battle that isn't happening.

Not yet, anyway.

But another force – the one we are part of – is emerging and the devil is defeated. In the real battle that is looming, Father's warrior angels and we will be fighting as a single unit that nothing can withstand. Actually, the angels are already here, frustrated out of their socks, waiting for us to get off our big fat pew and get our gear on.

There are less than one hundred people running the affairs of the world. You still don't see them nor hear of them but you can certainly see where they have been. These operatives have been following their agenda for more than 200 years and can even be traced back 900 years – and it is all coming together now at this time. It is an utterly satanic destructive operation. Some of you oldies, compare your nation now, to what it was like before WW2. The nation I live in now bears no resemblance to what it was even fifty years ago, let alone eighty. I do not like the new version.

All nations and cities and national institutions have this multi-pronged demonic force embedded in them and these are busily working at destroying their hosts right now. It is these manipulators who have already stolen the wealth of the whole world and have thrown the whole world into unpayable debt. They have already taken over the entire world oil supply. They are behind the governmental insanities, the massive drug cultures, the abortions, the murders, the incredible abominations, the stupid wars and their hideous weapons, world finance, inflation and bank plunder, medicine killing fields, the unbelievable insanity of the greenhouse gas, carbon emission, global warming, rising sea-levels scams, flu pandemics, panics and emergencies, financing Islam, abolishing the Christian church, killing Christians as a religious duty – you name it. They are going gang busters.

The tentacles of these entities have attached themselves to virtually the entire operation of running the functional affairs of the Earth in this day. They are creating as much confusion and mayhem as possible, and are doing a pretty good job of it. Then they will make a great show of coming to our rescue with all kinds of relief efforts – the intention being to end up controlling and owning everything.

Islam is invading nation after nation and governments around the world are so scared of them they are afraid to do anything about it for fear of retaliation. So they sit on their collective fannies and let the mob move in and take over. Armies from around the western world are right now in the Middle East trying to fight the devil with guns. They are such slow learners.

However, where iniquity has come in like a flood – expect a strong correcting force to undo the mischief they have caused. That strong correcting force is being prepared to show up right now.

All this mess is part of what Jesus and his Church – which is you and me – and Father and his Kingdom is being set up to deal with. We are being prepared to be part of the force that is going to overthrow these evil forces.

One hundred demon possessed men have created this current world turmoil.

One hundred Holy Spirit possessed men and women can fry their hide – and undo the mischief they have caused.

Let's do it.

It's God's people getting serious with God time.

It's becoming a duplicate of Jesus time.

It's Body of Christ time.

It's Kingdom of God time.

It's the Glory of God being turned loose on this planet time.

Let's do it.

I repeat – the critical mass is the group of Holy Spirit filled men and women who have wholly abandoned their personal agendas and ambitions and goals and plans and have allowed Holy Spirit to fuse them together with himself and with every member of the team.

That must happen, and until that happens it is not possible for anything to happen. Get hold of that.

The Kingdom, from within which The King rules, is wholly inclusive.

The satanic governments in the west are going. The Communist governments in the east are going. Islam is going. The Buddhists and Hindus are going. The Godless, lifeless, useless "christian" church is going. The genocidal idiot dictators and their militias infesting so many countries are going. The one hundred elite controllers and their interwoven tentacles are going.

There is a God in Heaven who has come to Earth with a mighty angel army to work together with us to get this job done. Together with God – **we can do everything**.

The nations we were told to disciple – not send missionaries to, but to disciple – but didn't – so Islam is doing it with car bombs – are ALL coming under the government of God Almighty, and I repeat, it is our responsibility to get these nations into the hands of Jesus, so he can hand them over to Father God, so God can once again be God over all.

And, as we work with our Father God in the restoration of THIS planet, he will be like a talent scout at a big game watching out for those who are showing Governmental skills and ability and stickability. Things are being made ready for the next stage. Eternity ahead is going to be very, very interesting.

On **this** planet, the intention of Father God from the beginning is that, as the result of this action of himself working together with us – **the glory of God will cover this Earth as the waters cover the sea.** Not just the "knowledge" of it, but the functional visible reality of it. And I intend to see that with these eyes in these days of my flesh at this time on the Earth.

And I am still learning and still being wholly intrigued – and yea verily – flabbergasted – discovering what God Almighty is really up to on this most insignificant microbe of a planet, infested by us sub-atomic human quarks. The situation is so bizarre. God is not logical.

And I am fully aware that what I am saying in this material scarcely touches the fringes of what is really going on in the background. God, and what he is doing is so impossibly huge we quarks haven't the capacity to even imagine what he is really up to. But it's going to be exciting to find out.

I have a lot more questions booked into headquarters that haven't begun to be answered yet – but they will be. There are so many things we have not been told and I think Papa wants us to know what he is doing so we can work with him to get things done. Some of that might make up another book.

And Father has his family.

Before the beginning of the beginning Father dreamed of having a family of sons and daughters who have matured to the point where he can enjoy intimate fellowship and intelligent conversation with us – and now we are here. Jesus has all these brothers and sisters he can spend time with – right down through Eternity. And Holy Spirit has all these grown up adults and teens and children – who don't stay teens and children very long – as the friends and companions he has been yearning for all these ages.

God Almighty has his family. We can talk with each other on the same level because we are *on* the same level and are *made to be* on the same level. We enjoy each other's company. We enjoy fellowship and companionship with each other. There are squillions of angels and beings of all types and classes living at Headquarters, but we are unique. We are different. We are duplicates of God. We are companions of Eternal Creator God. We are people who have chosen to love God because we want to – not because we are programmed that way. Our delight and joy is to have him as our Father, and Jesus as our big brother, and Holy Spirit as our friend and companion. We are **family.**

SO – sitting around in the family room at Headquarters, it is we who are the family. We chat with God and each other. We sip Celestial Coffee and munch angel cake. Sometimes we get serious and talk about the big government issues on Earth and out in Creation. From there we are trusted with responsibilities. We are assigned management posts with major development projects, both on Planet Earth and as we work with our CEO on Creation Stage 2.

Father knows he can depend on us. He delegates decision-making authority to us. We are big, grown up, mature, reliable, responsible sons and daughters, whose delight is to delight our Dad.

OK – let's have a Bible verse to make all this official.

"And all the people of the Earth shall see that you are called by the name of the Lord – **and they shall be afraid of you.**" Deut. 28.

There is an enormous adventure waiting for the man or woman who will choose to get real with God – God's way – and which will continue on and on and on and on......

Made in the USA
Charleston, SC
10 November 2013